A PASSAGE TO INDIA
Essays in Interpretation

A PASSAGE TO INDIA

Essays in Interpretation

Edited by

John Beer

BARNES & NOBLE BOOKS
TOTOWA, NEW JERSEY

First published in Great Britain 1986 by
The Macmillan Press Ltd

First published in the USA 1986 by
BARNES & NOBLE BOOKS
81 ADAMS DRIVE
TOTOWA, NEW JERSEY 07512

ISBN 0–389–20601–6 (cloth)
ISBN 0–389–20602–4 (paper)

Typeset by
Wessex Typesetters
(Division of The Eastern Press Ltd)
Frome, Somerset

Printed in Great Britain

British Library Cataloguing in Publication Data
A Passage to India: essays in interpretation.
1. Forster, E. M. Passage to India
I. Beer, John
823′.912   PR6011.O58P37
ISBN 0–389–20601–6 (cloth)
ISBN 0–389–20602–4 (paper)

Contents

Contents

Preface

Anyone attempting to formulate a unified 'theory of the novel' has to come to terms with the fact that different readers, faced with the same text, will read a very different novel. Each reader, according to training, temperament and present interests, will attend to particular features in the presentation and build up an interpretation based upon those.

A Passage to India is increasingly recognised as a novel which, answering to Forster's own complexity of mind, is rich in interpretative possibilities. In this collection various critics have approached the novel with a particular theme or interest in mind and presented a reading in terms of what they have found. The separate essays, each of which presents a coherent view of the novel from its own point of view, are followed by a Conclusion written in a more open manner, suggesting further perspectives which open out from the main lines of approach and mentioning examples of further criticism in each case. Students who come to the collection after studying Forster's novel will find in it both stimulating sources for discussion and a range of varying ideas from which to build their own patterns of interpretation. In some cases they will find it rewarding to look at what different critics have made of the same passage (whether they conflict with or reinforce one another) and to work on from there.

It is hoped that all readers of Forster will find interest in these pages. The appearance of a film based on *A Passage to India* naturally arouses a good deal of discussion, since a presentation which leaves out large and important sections of the novel must in one sense be a distortion. What a film offers, however, is a particular kind of 'reading' – a reading that is sensitive to the dramatic qualities and resources of visual imagery afforded by the text. Those who have written here on Forster's novel from the point of view of its documentary accuracy or its symbolism have relevant things to say about these matters; more often, however, it will be found that critics are complementing such an approach by their sensitivity to Forster's language, philosophy and narrative purposes. While giving a vivid sense of India and a sharp yet subtle commentary on British rule, *A Passage to India* is a meditative novel that reflects not only on the world but on fiction itself; even its language is constantly drawing the reader's attention to its own limitations and its own marvellous powers. These are qualities that a film can hardly touch on.

A Passage to India is an unusually rich example of what the novel can do. The approaches offered in the collection will therefore suggest possibilities for examining other works of fiction, helping to preserve readers and critics alike from the mistake of thinking that there is a single, 'right' way to read a novel of any complexity.

Acknowledgements

Chapter 3 is a revised version of an essay from *E. M. Forster: A Human Exploration*, ed. G. K. Das and John Beer (1979); Chapter 4 appeared originally in *Essays in Criticism*, xxx (1980) 151–66, and in *Approaches to E. M. Forster*, ed. V. A. Shahane (New Delhi, 1981); Chapter 6 in the *Journal of Narrative Technique*, ix, no. 3 (1979), and in *E. M. Forster: Centenary Revaluations*, ed. Judith Scherer Herz and Robert K. Martin (1982); Chapter 8 in the latter volume. Permission to reprint these items is gratefully acknowledged in each case. The other chapters were written specially for the present volume.

I am most grateful to Dr J. L. Fellows for providing the Index.

The volume first took shape in response to a proposal from the British Council's Literature Unit: I wish to express my thanks to members of the Unit, and especially to Yolande Cantù, for their interest and encouragement.

Key to References

Since a number of editions of *A Passage to India* are in circulation, all page references have been standardised to the later Penguin edition (Harmondsworth, Middx, 1979) which has been reset according to the Abinger edition of 1978 and is the one most readily available to students. The page numbers of each chapter there are listed below; this should enable readers without access to that edition to locate references fairly easily in the versions they are using.

The following abbreviations are used for the more frequently cited works by Forster: *AH* (*Abinger Harvest*), *AN* (*Aspects of the Novel*), *HD* (*Hill of Devi*), *PI* (*A Passage to India*). Page references to these works and to *Howards End* are given in the text, editions as specified in the Booklist.

Notes on the Contributors

Gillian Beer is a University Lecturer at Cambridge and Fellow of Girton College. She is the author of *Meredith: A Change of Masks, The Romance, Darwin's Plots* and a number of articles. Her latest book is a study of George Eliot.

John Beer, who is Reader in English Literature at Cambridge and Fellow of Peterhouse, is the author of *The Achievement of E. M. Forster* and joint editor of the collection *E. M. Forster: A Human Exploration*. In addition to books on Coleridge, Blake and Wordsworth, he has written articles on De Quincey, Dickens, Newman, D. H. Lawrence and others.

G. K. Das is Professor of English at the University of Delhi and is the author of *E. M. Forster's India* and joint editor of *E. M. Forster: A Human Exploration* and *D. H. Lawrence: Centenary Essays*; he has also published several articles on Forster.

John Drew, who has lived in India and lectured in Canada, was awarded a PhD at Cambridge for his thesis on India and the English imagination and has recently been teaching at the University of Singapore. He has also published a number of articles and poems.

Judith Scherer Herz, who formerly taught at Cornell and holds a PhD from the University of Rochester, is Associate Professor of English at Concordia University. She has written articles on Chaucer, Shakespeare, Milton and Marvell, as well as several studies of E. M. Forster, and is joint editor of *E. M. Forster: Centenary Revaluations*.

Benita Parry is the author of *Delusions and Discoveries: Studies on India in the British Imagination 1880–1930* (1972) and *Conrad and Imperialism: Ideological Boundaries and Visionary Frontiers* (1984).

Wilfred Stone is Professor of English at Stanford University and has taught at Harvard, Minnesota and Vermont, as well as at Stanford's overseas campuses in Britain and Italy. In addition to his writings on prose style and the short story, he is the author of *Religion and Art of William Hale White ('Mark Rutherford')* and *The Cave and the Mountain: A Study of E. M. Forster*, which won the Christian Gauss Prize.

Molly Tinsley teaches at the United States Naval Academy, Annapolis. She is the author of several articles and short stories.

1 *A Passage to India*: a Socio-historical Study

G. K. DAS

Critical scholarship on *A Passage to India* has shown that it is the socio-historical content which, more than any other aspect of the novel, has generated controversy. Enthusiastic comments have appeared, both for and against Forster's presentation of this theme, from the book's first publication until today (a cross-section of views will be found in *E. M. Forster: The Critical Heritage*, ed. Philip Gardner[1]), and it will not be an exaggeration to say that its wide reception over the years owes much to the author's extraordinarily sensitive handling of a major socio-historical event of this century, i.e. the dissolution of the British dominion of India. Several novelists from Kipling to Paul Scott have given us enchanting fictionalised pictures of imperial India, looking at it earlier in the century with pride, or later, as Britain's imperial possession was lost, with wistful nostalgia, but the distinction of *A Passage to India* lies in the fact that it registers the transitional moment of British India's transformation into a new India with a disenchantingly realistic and historical vision.

Forster's second visit to India in 1921–2 coincided with the momentous period of the Indian non-co-operation movement against British rule. The movement was launched jointly by the Indian National Congress and the Moslem League and was at its height of success during the months of Forster's stay in India. A 'resident Voltaire' at the court of the former Princely state of Dewas Senior, he was also a keen observer of the changing social and political scene of British India outside Dewas, listening to reports: 'the disciples of Gandhi used to . . . shout subversive slogans at us over the border' (*HD*, p. 63). If

1

Princely India seemed to Forster like Alice's Wonderland, the situation of British India at the time of Gandhi's non-co-operation movement proved to be one of complete disenchantment. The movement was an expression of India's protest against imperialism, social apartheid and repression, and Forster's accounts of it in the form of reports and the fictional representation of *A Passage to India* show the impact it had made on him. Rejecting the constitutional reforms of 1919, which gave the Indians an increased share of governmental power, the non-co-operation movement claimed complete social equality between the British and Indians. Its true spirit was expressed in the following statement contained in a public letter to the Duke of Connaught written by Gandhi:

> The non-co-operationists have come to the conclusion that they must not be deceived by the reforms that tinker with the problems of India's distress and humiliation. . . . We desire to live on terms of friendship with Englishmen, but that friendship must be on terms of equals both in theory and in practice . . . .[2]

Gandhi wished the Empire to be based on complete equality among its members, and his vision was identical to Forster's own conception of a 'democratic Empire'; when Gandhi published his open letter to the Duke, Forster also wrote in a similar vein of protest concerning the Prince of Wales's goodwill visit to India in 1921:

> If it crowned another work . . . if the subordinate Englishmen in the country had also been *naïf* and genial, if the subalterns and Tommies and European engineers and schoolmasters and policemen and magistrates had likewise taken their stand upon a common humanity instead of the pedestal of race – then the foundation of a democratic Empire might have been well and truly laid. But the good-fellowship cannot begin at the top; there it will neither impress the old-fashioned Indian who thinks that a Prince should not be a fellow, nor conciliate the Oxford-educated Indian who is excluded from the local club. It will be interpreted as a device of the Government to gain time, and as evidence of fear. Until the unimportant Englishmen here condescend to hold out their hands to the

'natives', it is a waste of money to display the affabilities of the House of Windsor.[3]

Protest against the evils of a colonial society is a dominant theme in *A Passage to India*. In the city of Chandrapore the British live like 'little gods'; socially they consider themselves superior to all Indians 'except one or two of the Ranis' (v, 61), and exclude the Indians from their club. The British official is given to hard work in trying to dispense justice and keep the peace, and thinks it his duty 'to hold this wretched country by force' (p. 69), while educated and politically awakened Indians question, 'How is England justified in holding India?', 'Is it fair that an Englishman should occupy a job when Indians are available?' (ix, 124), 'What is the use of all these reforms [an obvious allusion to the constitutional reforms of 1909 and 1919] . . . where the English sneer at our skins?' (xi, 128–9), and so on. Such was precisely the thrust of the non-co-operation movement, and the novel reflects the situation in remarkable candour. Forster, like Gandhi, had contemplated an India in which Indians and British might have lived as social equals. Both men valued personal relations above politics, and criticised imperialist policies of discrimination under which personal relations were vitiated. But while Gandhi had hoped that by launching the non-co-operation movement India might transform British imperialism into a happier institution, Forster believed the movement to have spelt the dissolution of British India altogether, and history has proved that his judgement was right.

There were two specific causes behind the non-co-operation movement: to seek redress for General Dyer's massacre of the nationalist demonstrators at Amritsar in 1919, and to protest against Britain's hostility towards the Islamic movement of the Khilafat. Forster was in full sympathy with both these causes. He condemned the Amritsar massacre as an example of 'public infamy' (*AH*, p. 23), and he disapproved of the British complicity in the situation concerning Turkey, the spiritual centre of the Khilafat. His whole approach to the non-co-operation movement demonstrates one important point: while this major movement in the history of the Indian Empire had completely baffled the British official mind, and hostile attempts were being made to misrepresent it, Forster looked at it not only with a remarkably accurate insight, but also with sincere interest and sympathy.

His full reaction to the situation surrounding the Amritsar massacre is reflected in the dramatisation of the actual events in *A Passage to India*. He uses these events to portray an important historical truth about the decline of British India, believing firmly that, if in the past policies of racial and social discrimination had weakened the structure of British India, the use of force and violence in the Punjab had further precipitated the collapse of that structure. Ideologically Forster disbelieved in force, and it had shocked him deeply that at Amritsar force had been exhibited brutally in the massacre of an unarmed crowd. In the troubled situation at Chandrapore, in *A Passage to India*, he telescopically focuses attention on the actual situation surrounding the Amritsar massacre. The connections between Forster's story and the actual situation are clear, although Forster seems to have deliberately avoided introducing the sensitive name 'Amritsar'. In the central episode of the novel which commences with the incident in the Marabar Caves, Calcutta and Lahore (places which, like Amritsar, were also full of unrest and tense political interest) are mentioned significantly as 'important towns . . . where interesting events occur and personalities are developed' (xiv, 148). The source of the trouble at Chandrapore, the alleged attempt by an Indian to molest an English girl, has a connection with actual events also. Fear was actually haunting the Englishwomen and their community living at Amritsar. Forster's description of the meeting at the club has a close resemblance with an account of Amritsar by 'An Englishwoman' published in *Blackwood's Magazine* in April 1920.[4] The author of this article, like Adela Quested, had arrived in India, new to the country. She was living at Amritsar at the time of wide nationalist demonstrations. She had personally witnessed the disturbances in Lahore, which had made her nervous, and now Amritsar was seething with unrest, and was unsafe. The bungalow in which she was staying had been chosen as a 'rallying-post for European women and children in the event of trouble'. She describes in great length how the mob had become violent, threatening to take the lives of Europeans, and how, in fact, a group of people had brutally assaulted an English girl called F. Marcella Sherwood, who had been living in Amritsar. With the help of some Gurkha troops this author and many others like her who were in panic managed to reach the Fort for shelter. There they found the atmosphere to be full of nerveless fear, closely resembling Forster's description of the scene at the Chandrapore club (xx, 187–93) following the alleged assault on Adela Quested in the Marabar caves and Dr Aziz's arrest. Since the authenticity of this particular scene has been challenged by Nirad C. Chaudhuri in his essay 'Passage to and from India',[5] I give below the eye-witness evidence of 'An Englishwoman':

> we saw smoke and flames arising from the city and heard that Europeans were being murdered. . . . About half an hour before sunset, news came that the Fort [Gobindgarh] was ready to receive us. . . . We set forth with some trepidation; but the arrival of some Gurkha troops about this time enabled the road to be picketed, and the way was safe. . . . [After arrival at the Fort] we found places where we could, and most of us packed into the upper storey of the 'Cavalier Block'. . . . A roll-call revealed 130 women and children, besides babies. . . . The outlook was not pleasant for women who had never known a day's real hardship before. . . .
>
> The days were monotonous and we had to keep very quiet for the sake of Miss Sherwood, who was lying between life and death. . . . After about a week it was considered safe for us to travel and arrangements were made to remove all the women and children to the hills. Special trains were run, packed with refugees from Lahore and Amritsar. It was considered better by the authorities that no women should be left behind, and they decided that Eurasians as well as Europeans should reside in hill stations for a time.[6]

Read alongside the above description, Forster's fictional portrayal of the scene at Chandrapore club shows a close parallel to the real situation at Amritsar. The general atmosphere of panic as well as many details of the actual occurrences are described in the novel authentically. The communal isolation of the British colony at Chandrapore, the hysteria about the safety of the British women and children (Forster's story of the alleged insult on Adela parallels the actual incident of the assault on Miss Sherwood), the civil administration's dependence on troops – especially the Gurkhas

– and the nervous dispatch of British families to hill stations: all these details unmistakably refer to the events of Amritsar.

The novel also refers to many specific atrocities suffered by the Indians at Amritsar, of which the massacre was the climax. An important clue to the real nature of these tragedies is provided by Forster's reference to General Dyer's 'crawling-order'. When the British community is gathered in Ronny's private room, adjacent to the court, to observe Dr Aziz's trial, Mrs Turton, the Collector's wife, remarks (upon Major Callendar saying that 'nothing's too bad for these people . . . there's not such a thing as cruelty after a thing like this'), 'Exactly, and remember it afterwards, you men. You're weak, weak, weak. Why, they ought to crawl from here to the caves on their hands and knees whenever an Englishwoman's in sight, they oughtn't to be spoken to, they ought to be spat at, they ought to be ground into the dust . . .' (xxiv, 219–20). One may read this detailed list of punishments for Indians suggested by an English District Collector's wife as comical exaggerations, but it will be seen that Forster's details are indeed a reminder of some of the most sordid punishments that had actually been inflicted on the people of Amritsar and other parts of the Punjab.

The full variety of punishments that had been imposed by the military authorities in the Punjab were reported in 1920 by a Committee of Inquiry presided over by the Scottish judge Lord Hunter. They were made familiar to the British public through discussions in Parliament and through detailed reports in some newspapers, especially in the columns of the *Nation*, where Forster could have acquainted himself with all the particulars. The 'crawling-order' was the most flagrant of these punishments. It had been imposed by General Dyer on account of the incident concerning Marcella Sherwood. Dyer had ruled that all Indians passing through Kucha Kaurhianwala lane, where Miss Sherwood had been attacked, must go on all fours. According to the Hunter Committee Report, the 'crawling-order' was issued on 19 April 1919 and continued in force until 26 April, and during that period about fifty Indians had been made to crawl through the lane. On the release in Britain of the Hunter Committee Report and the details of the 'crawling-order', it was condemned by some newspapers and also by the British Government, but it none the less remained as an irrevocable act in the tragic annals of the Empire, and in drawing

attention to it subtly in *A Passage to India* Forster underlines the
full depth of that tragedy.

In addition to the 'crawling-order', the novel also makes a
reference to public flogging, as had been carried out at
Amritsar, in the case of six Indians implicated in the assault on
Miss Sherwood. We see the Collector of Chandrapore sitting in
the smoking-room on the day of Dr Aziz's arrest, feeling the
impulses 'to avenge Miss Quested . . . to flog every native that
he saw' (xx, 190). Another purely humiliating punishment
used in the Punjab, the 'salaaming-order', is also cited in the
novel in a more elaborate way. The 'salaaming-order' had been
enforced so that Indians would, by law, show European officers
respect by saluting them. Proclaimed by General Campbell on
22 April 1919, the order was stated in these terms:

> Whereas it has come to my notice that certain inhabitants of
> the Gujranwala District are habitually exhibiting a lack of
> respect for gazetted or commissioned European Civil and
> Military Officers of His Majesty's Service, thereby failing to
> maintain the dignity of that Government: I hereby order that
> the inhabitants of the Gujranwala District shall accord to all
> such officers, whenever met, the salutation usually accorded
> to Indian gentlemen of high social position in accordance with
> the customs of India. That is to say, persons riding on animals
> or on or in wheeled conveyance will alight, persons carrying
> opened and raised umbrellas shall lower them, and all persons
> shall salute or 'salaam' with the hand.[7]

Fantastic attempts such as this to enforce subjugation on
the more independent-spirited Indians and to demand respect
for the British Raj are exposed in *A Passage to India* in the
peculiar relationship that is shown between Major Callendar,
the Civil Surgeon, and his subordinate, Dr Aziz. Summoned by
the Major to see him at his bungalow (ii, 38–9), Dr Aziz is
irritated. Reluctantly he cleans his pan-tinted teeth and rides in a
tonga to meet the Civil Surgeon. He is inclined to approach the
Major's bungalow riding in the carriage, but stops himself from
doing so, as that would have meant lack of respect for his
superior. Insubordinate habits of Indians, like Aziz's in relation
to Major Callendar, are also talked of later in the story by the
British officers: 'It's the educated native's latest dodge. They

used to cringe,' remarks Ronny Heaslop to Mrs Moore, 'but the younger generation believe in a show of manly independence. They think it will pay better with the itinerant M. P.'; in Major Callendar's view, the Indians did so to increase their 'izzat' (iii, 54), i.e. prestige. Still later, when Aziz has moved to the native state of Mau, free from the shackles of enforced servility under the British, he is shown, on one occasion, mocking the rules of British India such as the 'salaaming-order': seeing Fielding on an official tour in Mau, 'Aziz sketched a comic salaam. . . . Like all Indians, he was skilful in the slighter impertinences. "I tremble, I obey", the gesture said, and it was not lost upon Fielding' (xxxv, 296).

By 1921, however, the British authorities were in a greatly subdued mood. They were avoiding force in dealing with current popular agitations in order to avoid a repetition of the happening at Amritsar. Although there were demonstrations throughout the country by the non-co-operators, local authorities under the lenient policy of Lord Reading's government were forced to treat the rebels mildly. The Anglo-Indian District Officer, whose primary duty was to maintain law and order, was now, after Amritsar, required as far as possible to use methods of conciliation to get the co-operation of Indians in running the administration. Some officers found this situation odd, precisely as in *A Passage to India* the Collector feels amidst the crisis at Chandrapore: 'There seemed nothing for it but the old weary business of compromise and moderation . . .'. 'The dread of having to call in the troops was vivid to him' (xx, 190). Forster's fictional portrayal of the position of the British administration, faced by conflicts within the city and the situation precipitated by the incident at the Marabar Caves, clearly reflects his close analysis of the actual crisis in British India during the non-co-operation movement; his account also conveys his full reactions to the Amritsar massacre, which was in the background of that crisis.

The other important factor responsible for the crisis was the Khilafat agitation, on which light is equally clearly thrown in *A Passage to India*. At the root of the Khilafat agitation in India was the issue of Britain's prolonged hostility against Turkey. Indian Moslems considered Turkey as the sovereign land of the spiritual head of Islam, the Khalif, and their religious sentiments were intertwined with the destiny of the Khilafat (i.e. kingdom of the Khalif). Conflicts between the Christian powers of Europe and Turkey, therefore, had always had repercussions in India and produced Moslem resentment against the British authorities. Before the actual agitation in India, which began after the First World War, the attacks on Turkey by Italy, the Balkan League, and Greece during the years 1911–13 had aroused waves of protest among Indian Moslems against Britain's neutrality. Of the situation in 1913 (the date of Forster's first Indian visit), Lord Hardinge, then Viceroy of India, wrote in his book *My Indian Years: 1910–1916*, 'During the whole year there had been a certain effervescence amongst the Mohammedan population owing to the Turco-Italian war in Tripoli and the war in the Balkans.'[8] It will be remembered by readers of Forster that at this time Saeed, Forster's Moslem host at Aurangabad, had burst out against the British, 'It may be 50 or 500 years, but we shall turn you out.'[9]

Such periodic outbursts of Moslem resentments against the British thickened as Britain and Turkey became enemies in the First World War, and after the war, with fighting still continuing in Turkey, Moslem politics in India became firmly anti-British and agitated in support of the Khilafat. In 1920, as the Treaty of Sèvres was signed and large parts of Turkish territory were apportioned by the Allies, the Khilafat became a part of the non-co-operation movement, and at this phase the political union between Hindus and Moslems, known by the name of the 'Hindu–Moslem entente', was complete. Gandhi and the Khilafat leaders, Mohammed and Shaukat Ali, campaigned together for a common cause, against a common adversary. Protesting against the Treaty of Sèvres, Gandhi campaigned for *swaraj* [self-government] to be achieved through complete non-co-operation against the British. Mohammed Ali demanded aggressively (his words echoing in Dr Aziz's anti-British outbursts at the conclusion of *A Passage to India*) that the British must be driven out of India.

Forster had personally met Mohammed Ali in Delhi, and was well acquainted with the growth of the Khilafat movement and its conflicts with the British Government. Although he did not wish to support the Khilafat as an institution, he was strongly opposed to Britain's continued conflicts with Turkey. His thoughts on the Indian Khilafat movement and his criticism of British policy towards Turkey were publicly expressed in an article which he wrote on the subject in 1922, entitled 'India and the Turk'.[10] In this article he points to the pioneering part played by the Pan-Islamic propaganda of the Ali brothers, which had aroused among Indian Moslems a natural feeling of kinship with the Turk based on thoughts of the oneness of their Islamic faith and the greatness of their common Islamic culture in the past. Britain's hostility towards Turkey was thus quite naturally interpreted by Indian Moslems as anti-Islam, and Forster denounced it as an unnecessary evil.

The fictional portrayal of the political outlook of the Moslems in *A Passage to India* is to be viewed against this particular background. By the time Forster's novel was published the Khilafat had, of course, ended, but the revolutionary consequences of the movement in India remained permanently, and they had crystallised into some significant themes and conflicts in *A Passage to India*. The account of the transformation in the character of Dr Aziz who first 'took no interest in politics' (ix, 120) but later changed to the angry nationalist hating the British and, in fact, wishing in their place 'the Afghans . . . my own ancestors' (xxxvii, 315) reflects the way the Khilafat movement had actually influenced Moslem attitudes in India. Aziz is shown in the beginning as inwardly moved by the Pan-Islamic sentiment and by a deep feeling for the past glory of Islamic culture:

> the feeling that India was one; Moslem; always had been. . . . Whatever Ghalib had felt, he had anyhow lived in India, and thus consolidated it for them . . . the sister kingdoms of the north – Arabia, Persia, Ferghana, Turkestan – stretched out their hands as he sang . . . and greeted ridiculous Chandrapore, where every street and house was divided against itself, and told her that she was a continent and a unity. (ix, 119)

His pride of Islam flows deeply within his own private life without erupting to the surface as a political passion, and he finds fulfilment in writing poems about 'the decay of Islam and the brevity of love'. But once the British disgrace him and he is made their enemy, Aziz's racial pride asserts itself in the form of an angry political grudge against the Englishman. He assumes the uncompromising spirit of a Khilafat revolutionary: 'I have become anti-British, and ought to have done so sooner, it would have saved me numerous misfortunes', he declares to Fielding (xxvii, 250). 'Down with the English anyhow. That's certain. Clear out, you fellows, double quick, I say. We may hate one another, but we hate you most' (xxxvii, 315–16). Hamidullah, Mohamoud Ali, and even the loyalist Nawab Bahadur (he 'had financed the defence') all share Aziz's violent feelings against the English. Their unity reflects precisely the kind of unity that had occurred among the Moslems at the time of the Khilafat movement.

Turning to the Hindu–Moslem entente, we notice that all its peculiar ramifications too are reflected in *A Passage to India*. Dr Aziz's trouble unites the Hindus and the Moslems in the story. 'Another local consequence of the trial', we are told, 'was a Hindu–Moslem entente. Loud protestations of amity were exchanged by prominent citizens, and there went with them a genuine desire for a good understanding' (xxx, 264). In the trial Aziz is defended both by a Moslem pleader and by a Hindu barrister who is 'anti-British'. (It will be remembered that when the Ali brothers were arrested in 1921 for their provocative anti-Government speeches, Gandhi defended them publicly, and himself repeated the speeches as a way of protest against the Government action.) Aziz is acquitted by a Hindu magistrate, and finally leaves British India to take employment in the Hindu state of Mau. His 'genuine hatred of the English' prompts him to forget the differences between Hindus and Moslems, and he thinks, 'I am an Indian at last' (xxxiv, 290). The story ends with that note of Hindu–Moslem unity and the common political slogan, 'India shall be a nation! No foreigners of any sort! Hindu and Moslem and Sikh and all shall be one! Hurrah! Hurrah for India!' (xxxvii, 315).

In actual history, however, the 'entente' was a temporary affair. The general pattern of Hindu–Moslem relations in British India had been dubious in the past, and the Khilafat agitation provided a purely temporary bridge between the two communities. As Forster has rightly observed, their binding force was not constructive, consisting only in their political opposition to the British: 'As long as someone abused the English, all went well, but nothing constructive had been achieved, and if the English were to leave India, the committee would vanish also' (ix, 119–20). After their initial thrust against

the British, the Congress and the Moslem League again drifted
apart to express their opposition in their own separate ways.
While the Moslems claimed more and more separate privileges
for their own community, the Congress demanded a fully
democratic and a free India based on the abolition of communal
privileges. The religious differences between the Hindus and
Moslems sharpened their political conflicts, the effects of which
were several violent communal riots, and, ultimately, the
partition of India. Forster was well aware of these separatist
tendencies in Hindu–Moslem relations, and *A Passage to India*
throws light on this aspect in subtle ways. Aziz, and Das, the
Hindu magistrate, are shown one day after the trial shaking
hands 'in a half embrace that typified the entente'. 'You are our
hero', says Das, complimenting Aziz; 'the whole city is behind
you, irrespective of creed . . . .' Aziz remarks: 'I know, but will
it last?' 'I fear not', says Das, who, we are told, 'had much
mental clearness' (xxx, 264).

The discernment which comes across in Forster's
observations on the Khilafat and the Hindu–Moslem entente is
seen also in his depiction of the non-co-operation movement in
general. There are a number of intriguing allusions in the novel
to the actual progress of the movement. The incident of Dr
Aziz's arrest, for example, which (though apparently unrelated
to any political cause) is the main event behind the upheaval in
Forster's story, may be seen as a reminder of the numerous
actual arrests of Indians during the period of the non-co-
operation movement. In 1921–2, about 30,000 Indians,
including the Ali brothers, Gandhi and Jawaharlal Nehru, were
in prison. The outlook of the moderate leaders such as Gandhi
and Nehru had been revolutionised. On the occasions of their
trials both leaders made statements actually declaring the
sentiment Aziz voices after his trial, that they had lost their
loyalty to the British. Nehru, as reported in *The History of the
Indian National Congress*,[11] stated that ten years before he was
virtually an Englishman with all the prejudices of Harrow and
Cambridge, but was transformed in the space of ten years into a
rebel; 'We wanted to know you ten years back', Aziz announces
to Fielding; 'now it's too late' (xxxvii, 314). The organisation of
the Indian side after Aziz's trial closely follows the ideas and
strategies of the non-co-operation movement: the Hindus and
Moslems are united against the British; the Nawab Bahadur

announces that he should give up his 'British conferred title'; the students of the Government College are on strike and jeer in front of the City Magistrate's court, calling out that 'the English were cowards'; and Mohammedan ladies swear 'to take no food' (recalling Gandhi's method of fasts for public causes) until Aziz is released. 'A new spirit seemed abroad, a rearrangement, which no one in the stern little band of whites could explain' (xxiv, 218), comments Forster, and these words reflect the actual bewilderment of the Government at the time of the non-co-operation movement. In addition to these details, *A Passage to India* also draws attention to the strategy of a splinter group within the Congress, i.e. the Swarajists' policy of 'obstruction' – 'to kick and scream on committees', as Aziz thinks (xxxiv, 289) – and it anticipates extremist tendencies within the Congress such as those which were to grow after the non-co-operation movement, leading to the fiercer agitations of 1930–1 and 1942. When Aziz says, 'Until England is in difficulties we keep silent, but in the next European war – aha, aha! Then is our time' (xxxvii, 315), he in fact anticipates the extremist position the nationalist movement was to take in 1942, when the Congress withdrew support for Britain during the Second World War.

With all the strength of the non-co-operation movement, Indian nationalism had nevertheless two main pitfalls before it: the deeper communal rifts between the Hindus and Moslems, and the general opposition to the nationalist tendencies from 'native' India ruled by the Princes. *A Passage to India* throws light on the first element by drawing attention to the religious riots during Moharram, and it introduces the second through the theme of Professor Godbole's non-co-operation with Aziz's cause. When the Hindus and Moslems of Chandrapore have all combined to avenge Aziz, Godbole remains aloof: he is unconcerned by the fate of the Marabar visit and he leaves Chandrapore for the native state of Mau, his birthplace, 'to start a High School there on sound English lines, that shall be as like Government College as possible' (xix, 183–4), and be named after either Fielding or King Emperor George the Fifth. Godbole's aim is in contradiction to the spirit of the non-co-operation movement, which disapproved of Government schools and colleges and encouraged the establishment of national ones in their place. Viewed from the socio-political angle, his loyal outlook, and his aloofness from the agitation against the British precisely reflect the obscurantist spirit of Princely India.

Despite such limitations, the non-co-operation movement reigned over Indian social and political life from its commencement in the beginning of 1921 to March 1922, when Gandhi was arrested and imprisoned, and under its impact the Indian national movement acquired a shape and a strength of position which were not to be diminished under any future circumstances. The reasons for which the British ultimately gave India independence are of course various. But one major factor behind their decision was that their position in India had become unacceptable to socially and politically awakened Indians. The conflicts in British India at the end of the First World War had been proofs of that awakening and the non-co-operation movement gave it the character of a strong national agitation which worked with indomitable force till the end, successfully playing its part towards the dissolution of imperial India. *A Passage to India* presents this trend of events with remarkable perceptiveness and is fully alive with the spirit of the time.

Forster afterwards conceded to his Anglo-Indian critics that there might be some errors in the novel in matters of detail: bridge parties between British and Indians were no longer in fashion in the period, for example; a British Collector was not addressed as 'Burra Sahib' by his subordinates; Aziz's arrest without a warrant would be illegal. Forster also confessed to being unsympathetic to the Anglo-Indians as a class: 'how can I ever like them when I happen to like the Indians and they don't?'[12] He would further have conceded, one imagines, to his Hindu critic Nirad C. Chaudhuri, that a novel dealing with Indo-British relations should have had a Hindu rather than a Moslem protagonist. But what he did care to preserve truthfully in the book – and this is what makes it a distinguished creative work rather than a mere document – is the 'accent' of his own feeling rather than a strict adherence to facts. He realised that, even if he made certain changes, 'The facts might be right, but the accent would remain, and how on earth is one to do away with one's accent?' That he continued to feel more pro-Indian than pro-British he confirmed, some years after the publication of *A Passage to India*, in an interview with an Indian student, who died a Pakistani. At the interview, the student, a pupil of

F. R. Leavis (who had arranged for him to meet Forster, and told me the anecdote in a letter) said to him, 'It's remarkable how justly you hold the scales as between the Hindus and the Moslems. But there is one party you are *not* fair to!' Forster, obviously taken aback, said, 'Who?' 'The British', said the student. Forster laughed: 'Well, of course, one *can't* be fair to *them*.'

2   The Caves of *A Passage to India*

WILFRED STONE

At the centre of *A Passage to India* are the caves. In no book of modern fiction that I know is a symbolic centre so organically related to the whole as in this great novel. The caves are central both structurally and thematically. They provide the name for the centre part of this three-part novel and they provide the space – the poetic space, if you will – out of which emanates the novel's meaning. When Forster was asked in 1953 about the function of the caves in his novel, he said that he needed 'a solid mass ahead, a mountain round or over or through which . . . the story must somehow go'. He went on to say that he knew 'something important' happened in the caves and that 'it would have a central place in the novel', but he did not seem to know, at the time of writing, exactly what that place would be. The caves were an area where 'concentration' could take place. 'They were to focus everything up; they were to engender an event like an egg.'[1]

These statements reveal interesting intentions, if not very explicit ones, and they tell us unmistakably that we need to study the caves if we want to understand this novel. Just what was *concentrated* in the caves? What was the 'event' that they engendered 'like an egg'? What was that 'everything' they were to focus up? In this space I can only hint at answers to these questions, for the meaning of *A Passage to India* does not lend itself to paraphrase; more than most novels it has to be absorbed and contemplated, meditated upon like a mandala, before it yields its secrets. The most I can do is suggest what kind of mysteries the caves contain and how those mysteries are made known in the narrative.

16

What happened in the caves? On the surface level, of course, the 'event' engendered in the caves is Adela's panic – her terrified sense of being assaulted by something or someone. That terror fixes on Aziz as its object, and he stands accused of that consummate crime in the eyes of Anglo-India: a dark-skinned man attempting to rape a white lady. But did he do it? That mystery, intensified by the racial and religious tensions that accompany it, is the plot of the novel. It is a mystery that is not unravelled until Adela dramatically confesses, in the middle of the trial, that 'nothing' happened in the caves, that Aziz was not even in the same cave. These are the events that Santha Rama Rau concentrated on when she made a stage play out of *A Passage to India*; they are the kind of events that can be witnessed and acted out before our eyes, they are the kind of mysteries that can be *solved*. 'The plot', writes Forster in *Aspects of the Novel*, 'is the novel in its logical intellectual aspect: it requires mystery, but the mysteries are solved later on . . .' (v, 67).

But there are mysteries in this novel that cannot be solved, that have nothing to do with 'plot' in any usual sense, and that certainly cannot be acted out on a stage. When we ask what happened in the caves, we must ask about these other mysteries, for they are the mysteries that give this novel its essential meaning – even though we may quarrel about what, exactly, that meaning is. These are the mysteries of what Forster discussed in *Aspects* under the heading of 'Prophecy'. As plot-maker, the novelist is master-of-ceremonies, 'competent, poised above his work, throwing a beam of light here, popping on a cap of invisibility there' – but with the mysteries of prophecy the author is not the omnipotent or omniscient master-of-ceremonies but as much in the dark as anyone. (One can even argue that Forster did not understand the meaning of the caves, or of this novel as a whole, until years after he had written it.[2]) The mysteries of prophecy exist not to be 'solved', but to be wondered at, like religious mysteries – the mystery of the mass or of a medieval 'mystery' play.

The caves are rich in such mysteries, and the characters of this novel are tested by whether they can deal with those mysteries or cannot. Not all the characters of the novel enter the caves, but we can nevertheless say that some characters *can* enter them and some cannot. Mrs Moore and Adela both have traumatic experiences in the caves and are shattered by the mysteries they encounter there; Aziz, being Moslem and bored by most things Hindu, is a mere tourist to the caves and immune to their deeper significance; Fielding, that sensible 'holy man without the holiness', is curious about the caves as he is curious about everything, but he is baffled, and a little guilty, by his inability to penetrate them spiritually; Godbole alone, the devout Hindu, can enter the caves without fear and without evil consequences, for he is accustomed to wandering in such depths and caves are at the very heart of the Hindu place of worship. The Hindu temple is designed as a 'World Mountain', a tapering pile of stone with a cave-like sanctuary in the base, with a symbol for the sun at its peak, and on its sides heavy carvings depicting, as Forster writes, 'life in all its forms, life human and superhuman and subhuman and animal, life tragic and cheerful, cruel and kind, seemly and obscene'.[3] By a loose analogy, we can relate what is depicted on the exterior of the temple to what appears as plot in Forster's novel, and what appears in the temple's heart to what is allocated to the caves. Now this is not to say that Forster is a Hindu or that he is propagating Hindu values in this novel; but he is making the point that Hinduism is more open to certain kinds of experience than is Christianity or Islam, and that we of the West in particular are impoverished by our repression of the irrational and the unseen. The world of logic and common sense is there and it is important, but it is not enough – as this statement, written by Forster in 1914 after his first return from India, would seem to indicate:

Religion, in Protestant England, is mainly concerned with conduct. It is an ethical code – a code with divine sanction it is true, but applicable to daily life. We are to love our brother, whom we can see. We are to hurt no one, by word or deed. We are to be pitiful, pure-minded, honest in our business, reliable, tolerant, brave. These precepts . . . lie at the heart of the Protestant faith, and no accuracy in theology is held to excuse any neglect of them. . . .
   The code is so spiritual and lofty, and contains such frequent references to the Unseen, that few of its adherents realise it only expresses half of the religious idea. The other half is expressed in the creed of the Hindus. The Hindu is concerned not with conduct, but with vision. To realise what

God is seems more important than to do what God wants. He has a constant sense of the unseen – of the powers around if he is a peasant, of the power behind if he is a philosopher, and he feels that this tangible world, with its chatter of right and wrong, subserves the intangible. . . . Hinduism can pull itself to supply the human demand for Morality just as Protestantism at a pinch can meet the human desire for the infinite and the incomprehensible. But the effort is in neither case congenial. Left to itself each lapses – the one into mysticism, the other into ethics.[4]

Mrs Moore's rejection of 'poor little talkative Christianity' (xiv, 161) is evidence that she crossed, or tried to cross, this divide. But she cracked up in the process. Adela cracked up in a different way; more repressed, less religious, than Mrs Moore, she came with a desire to see the 'real India', but got more of that reality than she bargained for – or could stand. But for both – the tired old lady and the 'queer, cautious girl' – the transforming experience reached a climax in the caves, and for both it came in the form of an 'echo'. 'The echo in a Marabar cave,' writes Forster,

. . . is entirely devoid of distinction. Whatever is said, the same monotonous noise replies, and quivers up and down the walls until it is absorbed into the roof. 'Boum' is the sound as far as the human alphabet can express it, or 'bou-oum', or 'ou-boum' – utterly dull. Hope, politeness, the blowing of a nose, the squeak of a boot, all produce 'boum'. Even the striking of a match starts a little worm coiling, which is too small to complete a circle, but is eternally watchful. And if several people talk at once an overlapping howling noise begins, echoes generate echoes, and the cave is stuffed with a snake composed of small snakes, which writhe independently. (p. 159)

The echoes here are snakes and the snakes are echoes; echoes can strike the eye or the ear, or any other sense; they are capable of infinite synaesthetic variations, like the thousand manifestations of the Hindu god Brahma; and thus we are reminded that all the forms of the created universe spring from one source and can take an infinity of forms. For Mrs Moore this echo penetrated to the depths of her being and broke up the neat compartments of her accustomed values:

> The crush and the smells she could forget, but the echo began in some indescribable way to undermine her hold on life. Coming at a moment when she chanced to be fatigued, it had managed to murmur: 'Pathos, piety, courage – they exist, but are identical, and so is filth. Everything exists, nothing has value.' If one had spoken vileness in that place, or quoted lofty poetry, the comment would have been the same – 'ou-boum'. If one had spoken with the tongues of angels and pleaded for all the unhappiness and misunderstanding in the world, past, present, and to come, for all the misery men must undergo whatever their opinion and position, and however much they dodge or bluff – it would amount to the same, the serpent would descend and return to the ceiling.   (pp. 160–1)

How can we explain or understand these 'echoes'? At the time *A Passage to India* appeared, some of Forster's close friends – Leonard Woolf and Roger Fry in particular – criticised the novel for its 'mysticism'. Fry wrote, 'I think it's a marvellous texture – really beautiful writing. But Oh lord I wish he weren't a mystic, or that he would keep his mysticism out of his books.'[5] And Leonard Woolf, during a conversation in March 1965, remarked to me, 'Of course that cave business is all bunk.'[6] But Forster is not a mystic and the mystery of the echoes is not 'mysticism'; and these remarks are dramatic evidence that the gap between the Eastern and Western mind is as real and wide as the novel shows it to be. We do best if we go not to religion, but to psychology, for an explanation of the caves and their echoes. In Hindu mythology the caves represent the 'womb of the universe', from which, by some miracle of androgynous fertilisation, emanated all the forms of created life: first appeared a feminine principle (moon), then a masculine (sun), then the progeny resulting from the rape of the female by her offspring. There are many varieties of the myth, but basic to them all is the identification of caves with some primordial, prehistoric nothingness from which life emerged. If we seek a psychological explanation of the 'womb of the universe' idea, we can find a corollary in the psychological notion of the subconscious – or 'unconscious' as Freud always

termed it. Below the conscious mind is that depository of all that
the conscious mind has repressed or forgotten – of all that it has
censored or put out of mind in favour of the 'superego', that
agency of civilisation, culture, and morality. We can do no more
than invoke these familiar terms here, but Carl Jung's
understanding of the difference between the conscious and the
unconscious is particularly useful in understanding *A Passage to
India*:

> 'Spirit' always seems to come from above, while from below
> comes everything that is sordid and worthless. For people
> who think in this way spirit means highest freedom, a soaring
> over the depths, deliverance from the prison of the chthonic
> world, and hence a refuge. . . . The unconscious is the psyche
> that reaches down from the daylight of mentally and morally
> lucid consciousness into the nervous system that for years has
> been known as the 'sympathetic'. This does not govern
> perception and muscular activity like the cerebrospinal
> system, and thus control the environment; but, though
> functioning without sense-organs, it maintains the balance of
> life and, through the mysterious paths of sympathetic
> excitation, not only gives us knowledge of the innermost life
> of other beings but also has an inner effect upon them. In this
> sense it is an extremely collective system, the operative basis
> of all *participation mystique*, whereas the cerebrospinal
> function reaches its high point in separating off the specific
> qualities of the ego, and only apprehends surfaces and
> externals – always through the medium of space. It
> experiences everything as an inside.[7]

The unconscious is, in short, the inner cell of the World
Mountain, as the world of mind and will is its surface, and the
world of abstracting ideality the peak – or point of release. The
echoes of the novel demonstrate a *participation mystique*, and it
is just those people most resistant to the unconscious and most
devoted to 'the daylight of mentally and morally lucid
consciousness' – Adela and Mrs Moore and Fielding or Ronny –
who crumble or panic when the echoes invade. This is the
unconscious breaking into the conscious mind, and for one not
accustomed to such visitations it can seem – as it did for Adela –
like a rape of the personality. And the result, for Mrs Moore,

was a virtual abdication of the moral sense; she knew that Aziz was innocent, yet she did not lift a finger to help him, a religion of 'vision' having replaced her old religion of 'conduct' – and thus Forster tells us that neither one nor the other is, by itself, sufficient. After the trial, the citizens of Chandrapore are swept by a feeling of sympathy for Mrs Moore, and the cry 'Esmiss Esmoor' is the very voice of a *participation mystique*, the mob speaking as if in sleep or nightmare, and 'Esmiss Esmoor' is only 'ou-boum' at a higher level of sophistication and development.

The caves represent the unconscious in two senses – the repressed elements in the individual life and the survivals in modern man of the pre-historic and the pre-human, those elements that Freud termed the id. So that 'ou-boum' is something before language, a sound emanating from that dark, distant, prehistoric distance before language – and before morality. It is a time and condition that wipes out distinctions – all the distinctions on which Anglo-India built its culture and empire. That is why it is so terrifying: to lower one's guard before the primal forces of the unconscious is, to one trained in repression, nothing less than an abdication of all culture and a return to something like savagery. But that is not the way Godbole feels. When he sings his 'song without words', he experiences 'Ancient Night,' and that return for him is not frightening but renewing, for he knows those chthonic depths as a place of vision and inspiration rather than nightmare.

So we are now perhaps prepared to recognise the caves as a kind of echo chamber from which emerge echoes, like so many radio waves, out across the 'hundred Indias' to some ears that can hear them and some that can only resist them. These echoes – these emanations from the unconscious of mankind – come in an infinity of forms, as sight as well as sound, in seen as well as unseen form, as words and bees, as puns and divine visitations. When Godbole, in a state of religious ecstasy during the feast of Gokul Ashtami that concludes the book, 'remembered a wasp seen he forgot where, perhaps on a stone' (xxxiii, 283), and later in his rapt state remembers it in connection with Mrs Moore ('One old Englishwoman and one little, little wasp' – p. 288), he is remembering the same wasp that Mrs Moore, much earlier in the book, had seen and addressed as 'pretty dear' (iii, 55). These repetitions, these enterings of images into the minds of different characters at different times, and without any obvious causal connections, form the device whereby the collective unconscious manifests itself – and the aesthetic device whereby this novel is stitched internally and woven into an aesthetic unity.

But the echo of greatest importance is the repetition of the word and idea 'nothing'. On the very first page we are told that 'the city of Chandrapore presents nothing extraordinary' and as we approach the crisis in the caves these 'nothings' intensify: 'It so happened that Mrs Moore and Miss Quested had felt nothing acutely for a fortnight' (xiv, 145); 'There are periods in the most thrilling day during which nothing happens' (ibid.); 'Aziz noticed nothing' (p. 153); 'Nothing embraces the whole of India, nothing, nothing' (p. 156); 'Nothing evil had been in the cave' (p. 159); 'Nothing enrages Anglo-India more than the lantern of reason if it is exhibited for one moment after its extinction is decreed' (xvii, 174–5); Fielding 'experienced nothing himself; it was as if someone had told him there was such a moment, and he was obliged to believe' (xx, 197); Adela says, 'I know it's all nothing; I must be sensible, I do try –' (xxii, 204); 'What did this eternal goodness of Mrs Moore amount to? To nothing, if brought to the test of thought' (xxxvi, 306). The word is heard less often as the crisis passes[8] and the novel nears its close, for the echoes are most intense in the middle section; but throughout 'nothing' is both a presence and an absence, and those Anglo-Indians who experience 'nothing' are, of course, experiencing 'something' – they are receiving evidence that the unconscious exists and cannot ultimately be denied, however much it may be repressed. It is evidence that terrifies or puzzles them but is the very object of Godbole's desire. Perhaps one of the most pathetic scenes in the novel is that of Adela and Fielding trying to piece together the puzzle of what happened in the caves. 'Information' is one of Fielding's favourite words, as it is his faith that, given the correct information, all mysteries can be cleared up. Can Adela now say whether anyone followed her into the cave, now that the trial and the excitement are over? ' "Let us call it the guide", she said indifferently. "It will never be known" ' (xxiv, 261). But, they both agreed, Mrs Moore had known. How was that possible?

'Telepathy, possibly.'
The pert, meagre word fell to the ground. Telepathy? What an explanation! Better withdraw it, and Adela did so. She was

at the end of her spiritual tether, and so was he. Were there worlds beyond which they could never touch, or did all that is possible enter their consciousness? They could not tell. They only realized that their outlook was more or less similar, and found in this a satisfaction. Perhaps life is a mystery, not a muddle; they could not tell. Perhaps the hundred Indias which fuss and squabble so tiresomely are one, and the universe they mirror is one. They had not the apparatus for judging. (p. 261)

In that distinction between mystery and muddle, we get another set of echoes – and one of the clues to this book. 'Muddle' throughout the book is often a comic word, but it also describes a condition of separateness, of doubleness, that hints at everything that divides people and rives them into separate religions, races and political parties. Mrs Moore, after the caves, comes to a state 'where the horror of the universe and its smallness are both visible at the same time – the twilight of the double vision in which so many elderly people are involved' (xxiii, 212). Forster goes on, 'But in the twilight of the double vision a spiritual muddledom is set up for which no high-sounding words can be found; we can neither act nor refrain from action, we can neither ignore nor respect infinity' (ibid.). Earlier Fielding 'foresaw that besides being a tragedy, there would be a muddle. . . . He was not afraid of the muddle, but he recognized its existence' (xix, 183). These recurrences of 'muddle' are rememberings of a conversation occurring between Adela, Fielding and Mrs Moore early in the book:

'I do so hate mysteries', Adela announced.
'We English do.'
'I dislike them not because I'm English, but from my own personal point of view', she corrected.
'I like mysteries but I rather dislike muddles', said Mrs Moore.
'A mystery is a muddle.'
'Oh, do you think so, Mr Fielding?' (vii, 86)

Not to know the difference between a mystery and a muddle is not to know the unconscious from the conscious, and the inability of certain characters to make the connection is the reason for the tragic divisions that this novel demonstrates. For example, Aziz was 'endowed with two memories, a temporary and a permanent' (xiii, 140) and he normally relegated the caves to the former. And Adela had a 'double relation' (xxiv, 230) to the caves. But this novel is also fraught with a promise, or a hope, of unity; and if doublings characterise the things that divide, triplings remind us that there is a wholeness beyond these divisions. The book is interwoven with such trinities, from its most lowly and comic level to its most serious, from its basic structural level to its most metaphysical. There are the three races–religions (Moslem, Anglo-Indian, Hindu), the three seasons of the Indian year marking the three divisions of the book (cool spring, hot summer, wet autumn), the elements of animal–vegetable–mineral that contend for supremacy within these seasonal changes. Any whole view of the human predicament must take all these divisions into account, for Forster's vision of salvation in this novel is inclusive rather than exclusive – as shown when he has Mrs Moore, looking at the moon, feel a 'sudden sense of unity, of kinship with the heavenly bodies' (iii, 51) or when, at the final festival, Christianity is brought to book with the phrase, 'God so loved the world that he took monkey's flesh upon him' (xxxvii, 315) 'By sacrificing good taste, this worship [the festival of Gokul Ashtami] achieved what Christianity had shirked: the inclusion of merriment. All spirit as well as all matter must participate in salvation, and if practical jokes are banned, the circle is incomplete' (xxxiii, 286). The trinities of the book continually suggest this totality, sometimes in the very rhythms of comic triviality, sometimes in the rhythms of the cosmos itself. Thus 'outside the arch [of the heavens] there seemed always an arch, beyond the remotest echo a silence' (v, 71) is but an echo of the three arches of Fielding's house (vii, 81) or the three arcades (ii, 41) of the mosque into which Mrs Moore steps. When Aziz sees her there he angrily shouts (before he learns that she has removed her shoes), 'Madam! Madam! Madam!' (p. 42) yet from that rebuke their friendship grows, suggesting that the rift between the religions might be healed. Later Mrs Moore tells her son that what India needs is 'Good will and more good will and more good will' (v, 70–1) and some pages later Aziz echoes that sentiment in the sacramental chant: 'Kindness, more kindness, and even after that more kindness' (ix, 128). But anger as well as lofty sentiments are expressed in trinitarian form. Mrs Turton says to the men in the club, 'You're weak, weak, weak' (xxiv, 220), and Mrs Moore in her distraught state bitterly attacks love and marriage: 'Say, say, say' (xxii, 205), she said; 'Why all this marriage, marriage? . . . The human race would have become a single person centuries ago if marriage was any use. And all this rubbish about love, love in a church, love in a cave, as if there is the least difference . . .' (p. 207). And even the train carrying the visitors to the Marabar Caves goes 'pomper, pomper, pomper' (xiv, 148) as if in parody of that sacred OUM which the Hindu worshipper chants to evoke the god that may or may not come. All things, material and immaterial; all states of mind, kind and unkind; all peoples, high and lowly, must be included within the reverential embrace. That is not to say there is no good or evil, better or worser, but only that, if we are to effect our unity, or even to grasp the idea of unity, we must trace these echoes to their source – to that ultimate 'ou-boum' that makes known our common origin and the inescapable *participation mystique* of our final common resting-place. It is in this sense that these trinities are sacramental.

So 'mystery' in this novel does not emerge merely as something dark and occult out of the chthonic depths of the unconscious, though that is its origin. But out of that cave, and continually impinging on attentive and inattentive human consciousnesses, come those signals that tell us, whether we hear or not, that we are all in the same boat – not only we humans but, as old Mr Graysford and young Mr Sorley reluctantly discovered, wasps and oranges, cactuses, crystals and mud, and even 'the bacteria inside Mr Sorley' (iv, 58). In this day, aware as we are becoming of the interrelatedness of man and his environment, we can read *A Passage to India* as a kind of bible of spiritual ecology. It offers no solutions to the human muddle, but it offers a vision of what is involved if we hope to mend our tragic divisions, including those that divide us from nature as well as those that divide us against each other, and against ourselves.

3 The Politics of Representation in *A Passage to India*

BENITA PARRY

> Perhaps the most important task of all would be to undertake studies in contemporary alternatives to Orientalism, to ask how one can study other cultures and peoples from a libertarian, or a non-repressive and non-manipulative perspective. But then one would have to rethink the whole complex problem of knowledge and power.
>
> – Edward Said, *Orientalism* (1978) p. 24

> This pose of 'seeing India' . . . was only a form of ruling India.
>
> – *A Passage to India*, xxxvi, 301

I

The discussion on *A Passage to India* as a political fiction has for long been dominated by the followers of a mimetic theory of literature, whose quest for empiricism tied to didacticism is achieved when they find the narrative content to be an authentic portrayal of India and a humanist critique of British–Indian relations during the last decades of the Empire. Since the accession of critical methods concerned with representation as an ideological construct, and not a truthful, morally inspired account of reality, however, the politics of the novel have demanded another mode of analysis, where the articulations of the fiction are related to the system of textual practices by

27

which the metropolitan culture exercised its domination over the subordinate periphery; within this theoretical context, *A Passage to India* can be seen as at once inheriting and interrogating the discourses of the Raj. In common with other writings in the genre, this novel enunciates a strange meeting from a position of political privilege, and it is not difficult to find rhetorical instances where the other is designated within a set of essential and fixed characteristics: 'Like most Orientals, Aziz overrated hospitality, mistaking it for intimacy' (xiv, 154); 'Suspicion in the Oriental is a sort of malignant tumour' (xxxi, 276); and so on. It is equally possible to demonstrate that while the idiom of Anglo-India is cruelly parodied, the overt criticism of colonialism is phrased in the feeblest of terms: 'One touch of regret – not the canny substitute but the true regret from the heart – would have made him a different man, and the British Empire a different institution' (v, 70).

Yet to interpret the fiction as an act of recolonisation which reproduces the dominant colonial discourse would be to ignore – egregiously – the text's heterogeneous modes and its complex dialogic structure.[1] Even the most superficial consideration of the 'India' construed by Western texts, an India which was virtually conterminous with the European consciousness of it, will show that this canon of historical, analytical, propagandist and fictional writings (official minutes, political treatises, scholarly studies, geographical surveys, missionary tracts, journalists' copy, memoirs of civil servants and army officers, educational manuals, school text books, adventure stories, children's books, Anglo-Indian romances, the works of Kipling) devised a way of dividing the world which made British rule in India appear a political imperative and a moral duty. The strategy of discrimination and exclusion can be deduced from the series of meanings produced by the word 'exotic': dissimilar, unrelated, extraneous, unconformable, untypical, incongruent, eccentric, anomalous, foreign, alien, abnormal, aberrant, deviant, outcaste, monstrous, fantastic, barbarous, grotesque, bizarre, strange, mysterious, unimaginable, wondrous, outlandish. Only by wilfully suppressing its initiation of an oppositional discourse is it possible to insert *A Passage to India* into the hegemonic tradition of British–Indian literature.

Written from within the liberal–humanist ideology, and in its realist aspect using the style of ironic commentary and measured ethical judgement, the fiction does act to legitimate the authorised cultural categories of the English bourgeois world. Indeed, so far as it imitates 'the beauty of form . . . the harmony between the works of man and the earth that upholds them, the civilization that has escaped muddle, the spirit in a reasonable form' (xxxii, 278), the narrative organisation underwrites the value of Western cultural norms. Other rhetorical modes converge, however, to subvert the certainties of the fiction's own explanatory system as these are put into confrontation with foreign codes. It has been repeatedly alleged in the critical literature that Forster's India is an amorphous state of mind, a figure of inchoate formlessness, a destroyer of meaning. This is to substitute the firm stance on epistemology discernible in traditional fiction for the ontological puzzlement of a modernist text, where India's difference is represented not as a Manichean opposition threatening Western precepts and practices, but as an original system of knowledge and an alternative world view. Without embracing or consolidating the cosmic perspectives and aspirations institutionalised in some of India's major cultural traditions, the novel does, in its triadic structure of Mosque, Caves and Temple, undermine the politically constructed concept of India (as well as refusing the scented East of legend, and the India to be seen as pageant or frieze from the seat of a dogcart) to produce instead a set of radical alternatives to the meanings valorised by an imperialist civilisation.

Thus, within the novel's colloquy, the gestures of performance and force are countered by icons of restfulness and spiritual silence; the rhetoric of positivism, moral assurance and aggression is transgressed by the language of deferred hope, imponderables and quietism. Against the grain of a discourse where 'knowing' India was a way of ruling India, Forster's India is a geographical space abundantly occupied by histories and cultures distinct from the Western narrative of the world and the meanings this endorses. But if *A Passage to India* can be seen to act as an ideological catalyst, it can also be seen as constrained by its conditions of production. What is absent is a consciousness of imperialism as capitalism's expansionist, conquering moment, and the enunciated critique of the Raj is consequently toned down. Imperialism's triumphalist rhetoric is present, but modulated and made safe by irony. Lampooned in the conversations of the Anglo-Indians, it is without the danger such declamations arouse in Conrad's writings, where a language extolling might, force, domination and supremacy, conflating a mystical zeal for conquest with a utilitarian preoccupation with exploitation, engenders a ruthless criticism of imperialism's beliefs, practices and styles. All the same, given the evasions in the novel's articulations of imperialist ideology, *A Passage to India* is the limit text of the Raj discourse, existing on its edges, sharing aspects of its idiom while disputing the language of colonial authority. Forster's reputation as the archetypal practitioner of the domestic, liberal–humanist, realist English novel, has inhibited contemporary readers from engaging with *A Passage to India* as a text which disrupts its own conventional forms and dissects its own informing ideology. Where criticism has not applauded the novel's humanist political perceptions, it has scorned its equivocations and limitations; it should now address itself to the counter-discourse generated by the text, which in its global perspective refuses the received representation of the relationship between the metropolitan culture and its peripheries, and interrogates the premises, purposes and goals of a civilisation dedicated to world hegemony.

II

The symmetrical design and integrative symbolism of *A Passage to India* confirm Forster's wish to make a coherent statement about human realities through art – for him the one internally harmonious, material entity in the universe, creating order from the chaos of a permanently disarranged planet[2] – while the deeper structure to the novel holds open-ended, paradoxical and multivalent meanings, discharging ideas and images which cannot be contained within the confines of the formal pattern. In a text consisting of a political fiction, an allegory, a philosophical novel, a social tragedy and a metaphysical drama, both centrifugal and centripetal forces are at work: the themes diverge from the axis and realign, the literary forms radiate and join, the ostensibly poised whole emitting ambiguity, dissonance and contradiction which are formally repossessed and transfigured in an affirmative if allusive coda. The novel's mythopoeic mode strains after models of universal and ahistorical order, composing an archetypal symbolism intimating that there exists a metaphysical wholeness of all the antinomies in physical reality, social formations and the psyche. Countermanding this cosmic vision of vistas beyond the time–space world is a pessimism which perceives a universe apparently random and inhospitable to habitation, a disjunctive historical situation and the human mind divided against itself. The one orientation points towards an escape from the dislocations in the material world to the timeless womb of myth, the other confronts the present disarray in all its specificity and contingency. But finally, in the 'not now, not here' (xxxvi, 309), 'not yet, not there' (xxxvii, 316), another direction is indicated, one which forecasts that the visionary and the secular will be reconciled. This anticipation of a future still to emerge, a tomorrow radically different from what exists, is rooted in the belief that institutions are not inviolable nor is consciousness fixed; with this hope, the novel's metaphoric and realist modes merge, establishing that the flight into emblematic resolutions has been abandoned, and history reaffirmed.

Forster's nonconformity was evident in his distance from both the orthodoxies and heresies of British society. Though he shared the ideology of the middle-class milieu to which he was born, he was at crucial points disengaged from it, was a part of Bloomsbury yet apart, a socialist without doctrine, a reverent humanist reassured by the sanity of rationalism and the sanctity of individual relationships, who came to speculate on the satisfactions of sacred bewilderment and the dissolution of self in a transcendent other. With the accelerated disintegration of the old order after 1914, Forster's refuge in liberal–humanism, never wholly proof against the elements, was drastically damaged. Confronted by the breakdown in established values, the ravages of European competition, intensified class conflict within British society and growing disaffection amongst the colonial peoples, he looked outside England for a focus on this multiple disorder and, in choosing a route which passed from fiction centred on the condition of England to the global context created by imperialism, initiated a meeting with a defining condition of his times.

Forster has written of his visits to India in 1912 and 1921 as transforming experiences. For a small but significant number of

English writers, brought through circumstance or choice into contact with the colonised world, the encounter exposed their consciousness to rival conceptions of civilisation, culture and community, to cosmologies postulating variant orderings to the universe, other definitions of the human condition and alternative versions of personality structure. In negotiating the contrary modes of awareness, the divergent precepts and goals devised by the West and by India, Forster produced a novel which neither fully accepts nor entirely repudiates the standards and usages of either. The text reveals the crisis of liberal–humanist ideology – its impotence as a code in an embattled social situation where moderation and compromise are not possible, its inadequacy as an explanation of a universe more extensive than the environment made by human intervention, and the insufficiency of its insights into the potentialities of mind whose experiential range exceeds ratiocination and sensory cognition. Nevertheless, although the work ventures no affirmation of its creed, it is the product of an intelligence and sensibility nurtured within the cultural and intellectual context of liberal–humanism. It is because the novel is mediated through this world view and returns there for repose that the advance into new and profoundly astonishing perceptions is accompanied by retreats to the confines of known sterilities. The narrative voice oscillates between faith and disbelief in the validity of humanist mores, observing that, within an India divided into cultural groups not always sympathetic towards each other and ruled over by aliens hostile to all, community is both a refuge and a laager; that, if immersion in mysticism wastes secular proficiency, adherence to rationalism atrophies other possible facets of personality; that, whereas empiricism can provide a rigorous arrangement of appearances, it misses essences, and, if exclusion and definition lead to functional and aesthetic excellence, only the suspension of discrimination and the abolition of barriers will facilitate the making of a total explanatory system.

To these polarities no resolution is suggested, yet, because *A Passage to India* calls on resources outside the norms and priorities of Western societies, summoning other social configurations, ethical codes and philosophical systems, evaluations which have been made of Forster's 'medium mind' and his imprisonment within a superannuated system of ideas and values should be rephrased, for this novel both articulates in ontological and moral terms a radical dissent from the conventions and aspirations of the late bourgeois world, and omits to make the critical connection between these and the social and political structures they accompanied and sustained. Because of this, there is a vacuum at the core of the political fiction. Forster, always a cultural relativist, was amused at the rhetoric of a 'high imperial vision' and came to applaud the colonial people kicking against imperialist hegemony,[3] but just as liberalism was unable to produce a fundamental critique of Western colonialism, so is a consciousness of imperialism's historical dimensions absent from *A Passage to India*. Imperialism inflicted a catastrophic dislocation on the worlds it conquered and colonised, generated new forms of tension within the metropolitan countries and brought the West into a condition of permanent antagonism with other civilisations; yet about this very epitome of contemporary conflict the novel is evasive.

But if such elisions tend to disembody the criticism, suggesting an evaluation of a superstructure uprooted from its base, the British–Indian connection is nevertheless represented as the paradigmatic power relationship, and the encounters possible within the imperialist situation are perceived as grotesque parodies of social meetings. The chilly British circulate like an ice stream through a land they feel to be poisonous and intending evil against them; British domination rests on force, fear and racism, generating enmity in articulate Indians sustained by memories of past opposition to conquest and mobilised by prospects of the independence to be regained. It is the politically innocent Mrs Moore who challenges her son's brutal pragmatism with an appeal for love and kindness, a gesture towards humanising an inhuman situation, which is repudiated in the novel's recognition that hostilities will increase as Indian resistance grows (a process to which passing references are made) and British determination to retain power hardens. Aziz, the Moslem descended from Mogul warriors, and the Brahmin Godbole, whose ancestors were the militant Mahrattas, may have conflicting recollections of an independent Deccan resisting British conquest, but they are united by their distinctively expressed disinclination to participate in their own subjugation, a shared refusal which culminates in a Hindu–

Moslem entente. On the other side, the British make up their
differences and close ranks, with even Fielding throwing in his
lot with Anglo-India and so betraying his ideals.

The effeteness of liberal codes in the colonial situation is
established in the novel by the catastrophic failure of British and
Indian to sustain personal relations. The friendship between
Fielding and Aziz, disturbed throughout by differences in
standards and tastes, is finally ruptured when each withdraws, as
he inevitably must, within the boundaries of the embattled
communities, and it is Forster's consciousness that social
connections will fail which sends him in pursuit of spiritual
communion between Mrs Moore and both Aziz and Godbole.
But perhaps the most eloquent demonstration of liberalism's
impotence is its inability to offer any opposition to the enemies
of its values. The obtuse, coarse, arrogant and bellicose
deportment of Anglo-Indians, as realised in the novel, is the
very negation of those decencies defined through Fielding: 'The
world, he believed, is a globe of men who are trying to reach one
another and can best do so by the help of good will plus culture
and intelligence' (vii, 80). When Fielding, after his courageous
stand against his countrymen and women, aligns himself with
the rulers of India, he is submitting to the fact of imperialism,
deferring to a mode of behaviour and feeling made and needed
by an aggressive political system and conceding that his liberal
principles and hopes of doing good in India exist only by favour
of a Ronny Heaslop. Forster's tone can be mild, but the integrity
and toughness of his pessimistic acknowledgement that here
there is no middle way to compromise and reconciliation marks
a break with his previous, though increasingly hesitant, appeals
to rapprochement between contending social forces.

III

In an essentially speculative novel, intimating a universe which
is not human-centred and departing from the romantic
humanism of his earlier works, Forster – without relinquishing
trust in reason – reflects on the numinous as he perceives its
presence in India's religious traditions. The liberation to ecstasy
and terror of the psychic energies subdued by modern
industrialised societies, as represented in *A Passage to India*, is

significantly different from Forster's former domesticated exhortations to connect the outer and inner life, the prose with the poetry, for the sublime now contemplated has heights and depths never discerned in 'dearest Grasmere' or artistic Hampstead, and recognition of this augurs existential possibilities still to be assimilated by the West. 'Inside its cocoon of work or social obligation, the human spirit slumbers for the most part, registering the distinction between pleasure and pain, but not nearly as alert as we pretend' (xiv, 145). The awakenings of two Englishwomen dislocated by an India that confutes their expectations take cataclysmic form and result in derangement and delusion, the one mimicking in her feelings and behaviour the ascetic stance of isolation from the world but misunderstanding its meanings as meaninglessness, the other assailed by knowledge of sexuality and misinterpreting this as a sexual assault.[4] Both are negative responses to their perceptions of India's 'otherness': Mrs Moore shrinks the august ambition of quietism to the confines of personal accidie, while Adela Quested experiences cultural differences as a violation of her person. When the urbane Fielding has intuitions of a universe he has missed or rejected, of that 'something else' he is unable to know; when he and Adela Quested, both devoted to commonsense and clarity, speculate on the possibility of worlds beyond those available to their consciousness – then they are not yielding to concepts of heaven or hell, but (stirred by an India that is difficult, intricate and equivocal) recognising the possibility of other states of awareness.

What the novel produces in its transmutations of the numinous are dimensions to experience which are authenticated by their psychological truthfulness alone – expressing a hunger for perfection, a discontent with the limitations of the present and an aspiration to possess the future. The need for the unattainable Friend 'who never comes yet is not entirely disproved' (ix, 119), the yearning after the 'infinite goal beyond the stars' (xxix, 262), the longing for 'the eternal promise, the never withdrawn suggestion that haunts our consciousness' (x, 127), these are signs of that permanent hope which will persist 'despite fulfilment' (xxxvi, 299), just as the images, substitutions, imitations, scapegoats and husks used in religious ritual are figures of 'a passage not easy, not now, not here, not to be apprehended except when it is unattainable' (xxxvi, 309).

Significantly *A Passage to India* is a novel from which God, though addressed in multiple ways, is always absent – necessarily excluded from the caves of the atheist Jains, and failing to come when invoked in the form of the Hindu Krishna or the Moslem's Friend – the Persian expression for God.[5] As represented in the novel, the numinous is not divinely inspired nor does it emanate from arcane sources; it needs no religion and meets with no God. Forster's disbelief in the power of the human spirit to 'ravish the unknown' informs his transfigurations of the mystical aspiration:

> Did it succeed? Books written afterwards say 'Yes'. But how, if there is such an event, can it be remembered afterwards? How can it be expressed in anything but itself? Not only from the unbeliever are mysteries hid, but the adept himself cannot retain them. He may think, if he chooses, that he has been with God, but as soon as he thinks it, it becomes history, and falls under the rules of time.   (xxxiii, 285)

What Forster does acknowledge is that faith confers grace on the believer during 'the moment of its indwelling' (xxxiii, 282), and he affirms the gravity of religion's concerns, the fruitful discontent it speaks and the longings it makes known: 'There is something in religion that may not be true, but has not yet been sung. . . . Something that the Hindus have perhaps found' (xxxi, 274). This paradox signifies the meanings which Forster assigns the institutionalised routes to an understanding and changing of human existence devised by India's religious traditions.

IV

Theme and symbol in the novel's component modes converge on India. It is interesting that Forster's perceptions are in the tradition of Walt Whitman and Edward Carpenter, the one a passionate believer in popular democracy, the other a romantic socialist, both mystics and homosexuals disassociated by temperament and conviction from the conventions of their respective societies. Instead of the bizarre, exotic and perverse world made out of India by Western writers in the late nineteenth and early twentieth centuries, a compilation serving to confirm the normality and excellence of their own systems, Whitman and in his wake Carpenter found in that distant and antique civilisation expressions of transcendent aspects to experience and access to gnosis, predicting that, when connected with the secular, these would open up new vistas to democratic emancipation, international fellowship and progress.[6] But if Forster's India does have affinities with these poetic evocations, the perspectives in *A Passage to India* are informed by inquiry into, rather than new-found belief in, alternative ways of seeing, and the altogether more complex configuration centres on its difference and originality as a challenge to the authorised categories of Western culture.

It is as if the defining concepts of the major Indian cosmologies are objectified in the landscape made by the novel, and this presents to the alien a new awareness that humanity's place is within a chain of being linking it with monkeys, jackals, squirrels, vultures, wasps and flies, and on a continuum of existence extending to oranges, cactuses, crystals, bacteria, mud and stones. Drawing on Indian traditions, the text constructs an ontological scale situating the species in a universe indifferent to human purpose and intent, contiguous to an unconcerned inarticulate world, planted on a neutral earth and beneath an impartial sky. It is a position which seems to reduce existence to a respite between two epochs of dust, inducing a view of people as moving mud and contesting the centrality of human aspiration and endeavour. The Marabars, as a figure of eternity, and the distance behind the stars, as the sign to infinity, create mythological time–space, challenging the myopia of empirical observation and measurement. In the environs of the Marabars, where hills move, fields jump, stones and boulders declare themselves alive and plants exercise choice, hylozoistic notions formulated by archaic philosophies, and still extant in some Indian religious traditions, are confirmed. To the rationalist this failure to delineate and define, this obliteration of distinctions, spells disorientation and chaos; to the metaphysician it speaks of a continuous series accommodating disparate modes of being within one coherent structure.

It is this theoretical organisation of reality that is produced through the multiplex metaphor of India: an India which with its various cultures, religions, sects and classes, is difficult, arbitrary, intricate and equivocal, a microcosm of the 'echoing, contradictory world' (xi, 129), and an India which is the emblem of an organic entity, an all-including unity accommodating paradox, anomaly and antinomy. For if 'no one is India' (vii, 89) and 'Nothing embraces the whole of India' (xiv, 156), it may all the same be the case that 'the hundred Indias which fuss and squabble so tiresomely are one, and the universe they mirror is one' (xxix, 261). This possibility is translated in the gravitation of Aziz and Godbole towards a united front. Aziz attempts consciously to identify with India – 'I am an Indian at last' (xxxiv, 290) – and unwittingly becomes absorbed, as had his ancestors, in India; Godbole, while continuing to live obediently within the sects and castes of Hinduism, assists Aziz in moving to a Hindu Princely state and declares himself his true friend. But it is in the Hindus' ritual celebration of the entire universe of living beings, matter, objects and spirit taken into the divine embrace that the conception of a dynamic blending of opposites is symbolically enacted, that enigmas and contradictions are ceremonially resolved and fusion is abstractly attained.

Although he was not a scholar of Indian metaphysics, Forster was familiar with the myths, epics and iconography of India's varied cultures and found their innately dialectical style congenial. On rereading the *Bhagavad-Gita* in 1912 before his first visit to India, he noted that he now thought he had got hold of it: 'Its division of states into Harmony Motion Inertia (Purity Passion Darkness).'[7] These three qualities, constituting in the classical Indian view the very substance of the universe,[8] are permuted in *A Passage to India* as Mosque, Caves and Temple, a sequence with multiple meanings – one of which is the ontological and psychological significance pertaining to three major Indian philosophical–religious systems: they are figures, respectively, of consciousness and the present, the unconscious and the past, and the emergent metaconsciousness and the future. The novel offers this triad as the form of differences contained within a whole: incorporated in the enclosing frame is the gracious culture of Islam in India, a society where personal relations amongst Moslems do flourish; the unpeopled Jain caves, place of the ascetic renunciation of the world; and the buoyant religious community of the Hindus, internally divided and internally cohesive. The approach to the component meanings of these systems is, however, profoundly ambiguous, moving between responsiveness and rejection, making the myth and subverting it.

Mystical Sufi tendencies are represented in the unmistakably Indian incarnation of Islam, a monotheistic and historically recent religion, dually committed to the mundane and the sacred. But, having confronted the more ambitious theories of older India, Forster now relegates Islam's consummation of the prose–poetry connection as too symmetrical, shallow and easy. With 'Caves', the novel passes back to the world-rejecting atheist tradition of the Jains,[9] a post-Vedic heterodoxy of the fifth century BC but, like Buddhism – with which it has historical and theoretical affinities – rooted in the ancient, aboriginal metaphysics of primal, Dravidian India. Here the novel produces a version of this uncompromisingly pessimistic outlook, one which disparages bondage to the phenomenal universe as the source of pain and suffering, and pursues liberation from all involvement with matter. The contemplation of negatives and Nothing within the text culminates in the transfiguration of the ascetic world view, and, if 'Everything exists, nothing has value' (xiv, 160) is a statement of nihilism, it has an alternative meaning, one which acknowledges the material world as verifiable but assigns significance only to Nothing, to complete detachment: 'Nothing is inside them, they were sealed up before the creation of pestilence or treasure; if mankind grew curious and excavated, nothing, nothing would be added to the sum of good and evil' (xii, 139).

There is a striking ambivalence to the imagery of the Caves; their 'internal perfection' is evoked through crystalline figures of pure emptiness. But competing with and countermanding the delicate transparency of their interiors is the opaque menace of their external form:

There is something unspeakable in these outposts. They are like nothing else in the world and a glimpse of them makes the breath catch. They rise abruptly, insanely, without the proportion that is kept by the wildest hills elsewhere, they bear no relation to anything dreamt or seen. To call them 'uncanny' suggests ghosts, and they are older than all spirit. (xii, 137)

This speaks of the formless, primordial abyss before time and space, threatening to overwhelm consciousness, an enunciation which undermines the representation of Nothing as an authentic negative aspiration.

Moving forward to the Hinduism of India's Aryan invaders, the novel represents that tradition's ecstatic affirmation of the entire world, the ceremonial celebration of all matter and spirit as originating from and sharing in the Lord of the Universe. But if the text participates in the ambition of Hinduism – itself compounded over aeons through the assimilation and reworking of many other existing beliefs – to tie, weld, fuse and join all the disparate elements of being and existence in a complete union, it withdraws from the incalculable and unassimilable enormity of the enterprise. While *A Passage to India* applauds the refusal of the present as it is, the wish to supersede all obstacles in the way of wholeness, it rejects emblematic resolutions. The impulse to the ceremonies is shown as magnificent:

> Infinite Love took upon itself the form of SHRI KRISHNA, and saved the world. All sorrow was annihilated, not only for Indians, but for foreigners, birds, caves, railways, and the stars; all became joy, all laughter; there had never been disease nor doubt, misunderstanding, cruelty, fear. (xxxiii, 285)

But when the celebrations end, the divisions and confusions of daily life return. Just as consciousness of political conflict and social divergence transgresses against the will to union, so is there here a humanist's repudiation of symbolic concord. The allegory is over before the novel ends, the aesthetic wholeness dismembered by the fissures and tensions of the disjoint, prosaic world that the novel represents; the permanent is dissolved in the acid of contingency. In the last pages emblems of reconciliation and synthesis compete with their opposites: 'the scenery, though it smiled, fell like a gravestone on any human hope' (xxxvii, 315). The illimitable aspiration is not consummated: 'a compromise had been made between destiny and desire, and even the heart of man acquiesced' (xxxvi, 302).

V

In retrospect it is apparent that the authority of the allegory is throughout undermined by other modes within the text; as each positing of universal abstractions is countermanded by perceptions of the specifics in the historical situation, so the cosmic is cut down to size by the comic – the squeals of a squirrel, though 'in tune with the infinite, no doubt' (x, 126), are not attractive except to other squirrels; trees of poor quality in an inferior landscape call in vain on the absolute, for there is not enough God to go round; there are gods so universal in their attributes that they 'owned numerous cows, and all the betel-leaf industry, besides having shares in the Asirgarh motor-omnibus' (xxxv, 294), and a god whose love of the world had impelled him to take monkey flesh upon himself. From the infinite the novel returns to the ordinary; from eternity there is a bridge back to the mundane. The worth of human effort, ingenuity and creativity is restored in the view Mrs Moore has on her last journey across India, where the symbolic landscape is pervaded by history and culture:

> She watched the indestructible life of man and his changing faces, and the houses he had built for himself and God. . . . She would never visit Asirgarh or the other untouched places; neither Delhi nor Agra nor the Rajputana cities nor Kashmir, nor the obscurer marvels that had sometimes shone through men's speech: the bilingual rock of Girnar, the statue of Shri Belgola, the ruins of Mandu and Hampi, temples of Khajuraho, gardens of Shalimar.   (xxiii, 213–14)

The balance is redressed, and in the retreat to the Mediterranean it is overturned in favour of the secular and the 'normal'. The relief and pleasure known by both Adela Quested and Fielding on their return voyages from India is confirmed by that narrative voice which has throughout posited and endorsed Western norms and values; and the paean to Venice is eloquent of an ambivalence within the text's discourse towards the alternatives it poses:

> the harmony between the works of man and the earth that upholds them, the civilisation that has escaped muddle, the

spirit in a reasonable form. . . . The Mediterranean is the human norm. When men leave that exquisite lake, whether through the Bosphorus or the Pillars of Hercules, they approach the monstrous and extraordinary; and the southern exit leads to the strangest experience of all.   (xxxii, 278)

But neither this tenuous repose nor the symbolic solutions, neither the inevitability of compromise nor the permanence of conflict is the final word, for these are superseded by the generation of hope in a future when the obstacles the novel has confronted will have been overcome in history. On their last ride together, Aziz and Fielding, after misunderstanding, bitterness and separation, are friends again 'yet aware that they could meet no more' (xxxvii, 310), that 'socially they had no meeting place' (p. 312). But Aziz, anticipating the time of freedom from imperialist rule, promises, 'and then . . . you and I shall be friends' (p. 316); and when Fielding asks why this cannot be now, earth, creatures and artefacts intercede to reject the possibility: 'they didn't want it, they said in their hundred voices, "No, not yet", and the sky said, "No, not there." '

A Passage to India is Forster's epitaph to liberal–humanism. In search of other systems he had contemplated traditions to which ironically he had access because of the global space created and divided by imperialism, and if he withdrew from the sheer magnitude of the ambition to liberation nurtured within Indian philosophical modes, he had acquired a perspective on a transfigured tomorrow that made the social hope of his earlier fictions seem parochial. But as fascism, persecution, war and the repression of the colonial struggle brought force and violence near and made the 'not yet' seem ever more distant, Forster retired to essays, criticism, biography and broadcasts, media in which it was still possible to reiterate an adherence to liberal values, an option unavailable in self-interrogating fictional texts. In 1935 Forster attended the International Association of Writers for the Defence of Culture in Paris, a meeting organised by the Popular Front to unite communists, socialists and liberals in defence of 'the cultural heritage'. It is possible in retrospect to be cynical about the political humanism which the congress opportunistically advocated and to observe that Forster would have been quite at home in such a gathering. At the time it was surely an act of integrity by an untheoretical socialist determined to demonstrate his opposition to fascism. In his address Forster used the vocabulary of liberalism – justice, culture, liberty, freedom – and conceded that the times demanded another language which he could not speak:

> I know very well how limited, and how open to criticism, English freedom is. It is race-bound and it's class-bound . . . you may have guessed that I am not a Communist, though perhaps I might be one if I was a younger and a braver man, for in Communism I can see hope. It does many things which I think evil, but I know that it intends good. I am actually what my age and my upbringing have made me – a bourgeois who adheres to the British constitution, adheres to it rather than supports it . . . .[10]

Forster needed no critics to tell him of the ambiguities, contradictions and limitations in his intellectual stance; brought to *A Passage to India*, such categories reveal the constraints on the text's system of representation – an analysis which should not hinder the perception that this novel is a rare instance of a libertarian perspective on another and subordinated culture produced from within an imperialist metropolis.[11]

4 Negation in *A Passage to India*

GILLIAN BEER

Much recent narrative theory has impressed on us the significance of gaps, fissures, absences and exclusions in the composition of a fiction and in our reading and our judgement of it. We have also been reminded of the essentially linguistic nature of the novel and attention has shifted from character to language, to the text as process rather than the text as memory. It is in memory that the discussion of character thrives. Linguistic process is the reader's experience only while he is reading. But since the novel, as opposed to folktale, is an invariant linguistic structure composed by a single author, the order of its words is the condition of receiving its experience. Forster himself emphasised the act of reading in *Aspects of the Novel*.

> Books have to be read (worse luck, for it takes a long time); it is the only way of discovering what they contain. A few savage tribes eat them, but reading is the only form of assimilation revealed to the West. The reader must sit down alone and struggle with the writer, and this the pseudo-scholar will not do. He would rather relate a book to the history of its time, to events in the life of the author, to the events it describes, above all to some tendency . . . in the rather ramshackly course that lies ahead of us, we cannot consider fiction by periods, we must not contemplate the stream of time. Another image better suits our powers: that of all the novelists writing their novels at once . . . they all hold pens in their hands, and are in the process of creation.   (i, 8)

The insistent ahistoricism of this passage allies him unexpectedly in this at least with writers such as Propp and Jolles (who, incidentally, and paradoxically, were writing in the same historical period).

Readers must read, alone, and writers hold pens in their hands. Although Forster gives little direct attention to the language of fiction in *Aspects*, he asserts that characters in a novel are 'word-masses' and that a central topic must be 'the relation of characters to the other aspects of the novel' (iii, 30–1).

Coming to Forster's *A Passage to India* again after a long period I found myself alerted to properties of the work which seemed at first almost too simply to confirm what Macherey, say, or Iser (in *The Act of Reading*) had been telling us. *A Passage to India* is, after all, a book *about* gaps, fissures, absences, and exclusions: about bridge parties that don't bridge, about caves broached by man-made entrances, about absent witnesses who do not witness and who are indeed already dead, about events which may or may not have occurred, about how society – how meaning itself – depends upon exclusion: 'We must exclude someone from our gathering, or we shall be left with nothing' (iv, 58).

Negative sentence structures, together with the words, 'no', 'not', 'never' and in particular 'nothing', predominate in the linguistic ordering of this novel. This is so to an extent that goes beyond the possibility of 'accident', far beyond the language of Forster's other novels. Nor can the insistent negativity be read simply as an unmediated representation of a particular class vernacular of the 1910s and 1920s. Although it does draw upon habitual understatement and irony, it dislodges the assumptions embedded in such locutions. My first presumption on realising how frequent negative structures and vocabulary were in this text was that this would provide an inert and invariable medium of experience for the reader which would persistently controvert the book's topic: the will towards friendship and relationship. But as I moved further through the text I came to see that the uses of negation were themselves changing as the book went on. The function I had first noted is itself undermined before the book concludes. The shifting significance of negation in *A Passage to India* both challenges the older reading of the novel as essentially liberal–humanist, preoccupied with human personality, and raises questions concerning the Machereyan concept of the text as precipitated *communal* ideology: 'tout ce qui n'était que pressentiment collectif, projet, aspiration, précipite brusquement dans une image vite familière, qui devient alors pour nous la réalité, la chair même de ces projets, cela qui leur donne réalité'.[1] So far as this text is ideological, it is an ideology which manifests itself as space – the space between cultures, the space beyond the human, the space which can never be sufficiently filled by aspiration or encounter. The presence of negative elements in the syntax of a sentence does not in itself necessarily enforce negation. However the nominalised form 'nothing' remains always significantly negative whether or not its force as negation is confirmed grammatically. The frequent use of the word 'nothing' in *A Passage to India* therefore supports my general argument that negation has ideological significance in this work.[2] Negation and negativity in this novel are related in complex ways to place and space (interiority and exteriority) and to the diverse shapes of inclusion and exclusion supposed by the different religious orderings of life.

The book opens with a description which negates even as it creates picturesque images. The whole opens with a phrase of exclusion – which is extended as absence:

> Except for the Marabar Caves – and they are twenty miles off – the city of Chandrapore presents *nothing extraordinary*. Edged rather than washed by the river Ganges, it trails for a couple of miles along the bank, *scarcely distinguishable* from the rubbish it deposits so freely. There are *no* bathing steps on the river front, as the Ganges happens *not* to be holy here; indeed there is *no* river front, and the bazaars *shut out* the wide and shifting panorama of the stream. . . . The zest for decoration stopped in the eighteenth century, *nor* was it ever democratic. There is *no* painting and *scarcely any* carving in the bazaars. . . . Houses do fall, people are drowned and left rotting, but the general outline of the town persists, swelling here, shrinking there, like some low but indestructible form of life.   (i, 31; emphasis added)

At the end of the paragraph the main clause of the sentence thrusts through to the positive ('Houses *do* fall, people *are* drowned') while the sense registers decadence and mortality. The book closes in this way:

> But the horses didn't want it – they swerved apart; the earth didn't want it, sending up rocks through which riders must pass single-file; the temples, the tank, the jail, the palace, the birds, the carrion, the Guest House, that came into view as they issued from the gap and saw Mau beneath: they didn't want it, they said in their hundred voices 'No, not yet', and the sky said, 'No, not there.'   (xxxvii, 316)

Negation persists, and though cast in abridged form ('didn't') it is reiterated. The final negatives are localised in particular time and particular space: ('not yet', 'not there'). Since the book ends here, the negatives are given the authority of conclusion, but neither of them is absolute or universal. Other times, other places, are not entirely obliterated, but neither are they released into that which can be told within the book.

I am not claiming that negative forms are always significantly placed and used wherever they occur throughout the book – far from it. Indeed that is part of the point. For a good deal of our awkward and testing journey through the reading of this text, negative sentence structures, and words such as 'no', 'not', 'scarcely', 'barely', though omnipresent are unemphatically there, hardly registered. They are *even* rather than cumulative in their effect, rarely releasing us into any kind of crisis. Negation is not used only at particularly significant moments: it is used everywhere. The factitious and the significant both find negative forms; and these forms occur both in dialogue and narrative. The following examples are all taken from chapter viii. I could have repeated this demonstration of the frequency of negative forms from any chapter of the book, as the reader will find.

> Ronny laughed with restraint. *He did not approve* of English people taking service under the native States, where they obtain a certain amount of influence, but *at the expense of* the general prestige. The humorous triumphs of a freelance are *of no assistance* to an administrator, and he told the young lady that she would outdo Indians at their own game if she went on much longer.

'They always sack me before that happens, and then I get another job. The whole of India seethes with Maharanis and Ranis and Begums who clamour for such as me.'

'Really. *I had no idea.*'

'How could you have any idea, Mr Heaslop? What should he know about Maharanis, Miss Quested? *Nothing. At least I should hope not.*'

'I understand those big people *are not particularly interesting*', said Adela quietly, disliking the young woman's tone.   (p. 107; emphasis added)

The negatives here are supplemented by 'with restraint', 'quietly', 'disliking' – all expressive of rejection or constraint. Some pages further on comes the account of the accident with an unknown animal which involved 'no great crimes', 'Nothing; no one hurt,' 'nothing criminal' and Krishna the peon who has 'not turned up'. 'Ronny stormed, shouted, howled and only the experienced observer could tell that *he was not angry, did not much want the files*, and *only made a row* because it was the custom.' The experienced observers here are the servants in addition to narrator and reader. The chapter ends with Miss Quested and Mrs Moore playing patience and the last sentences are these:

Presently the players went to bed, but *not before* other people had woken up elsewhere, people whose emotions they *could not share, and whose existence they ignored. Never tranquil, never perfectly dark*, the night wore itself away, distinguished from other nights by two or three blasts of wind, which seemed to fall perpendicularly out of the sky and to bounce back into it, hard and compact, *leaving no freshness behind them*: the Hot Weather was approaching.   (p. 114; emphasis added)

In this passage a topic is expressed which elsewhere declares itself syntactically as well as in vocabulary: the topic of *alternation* with its conjoined ideas, incompleteness and endlessness. I shall return to this point.

The use of negative forms opens constantly towards indeterminacy. To say what something is *not* leaves open a very great area of what it might be. Such negatives are the most grudging form of identification and emphasise the extent of what is unsaid, or indescribable: take for example the first extended discussion of the Marabar Caves, between Adela Quested and Dr Godbole:

> 'Are they large caves?' she asked.
> 'No, not large.'
> 'Do describe them, Professor Godbole.'
> 'It will be a great honour.' . . . After an impressive pause he said: 'There is an entrance in the rock which you enter, and through the entrance is the cave.'
> 'Something like the caves at Elephanta?'
> 'Oh no, not at all; at Elephanta there are sculptures of Siva and Parvati. There are no sculptures at Marabar.'
> 'They are immensely holy, no doubt', said Aziz, to help on the narrative.
> 'Oh no, oh no.'
> 'Still, they are ornamented in some way.'
> 'Oh no.'
> 'Well, why are they so famous? We all talk of the famous Marabar Caves. Perhaps that is our empty brag.'
> 'No, I should not quite say that.'
> 'Describe them to this lady, then.'
> 'It will be a great pleasure.' He forewent the pleasure, and Aziz realised that he was keeping back something about the caves . . . .   (vii, 91–2)

As the book goes on, we discover that Aziz was right only in a broader sense – Godbole was not concealing *something*, but *nothing*.

'Nothing' is a word of power in this text. The theme of nothing is carried for a long time lexically, emerging only intermittently and later into action or character or landscape. It occurs in the first sentence of the book. I quoted earlier the end of chapter iv: 'We must exclude someone from our gathering, or we shall be left with nothing.' From that point on, the word occurs with increasing frequency. It is crucial in the scene where Adela first breaks off her engagement to Ronny and is there associated with all that resists identification. Adela, heavily feeling the absence of 'a profound and passionate speech', reiterates the words 'nothing else' while absently watching a neat and brilliant bird. She asks Ronny to identify it:

> 'Bee-eater.'
> 'Oh no, Ronny, it has red bars on its wings.'
> 'Parrot,' he hazarded.
> 'Good gracious, no.'
> The bird in question dived into the dome of the tree. It was of no importance, yet they would have liked to identify it, it would somehow have solaced their hearts. But nothing in India is identifiable, the mere asking of a question causes it to disappear or to merge in something else.   (viii, 101)

This escape from question and identification is repeated in the lies of the Indian characters, which open ways towards what might be, what may be wished, what might have been, routes out of the determined. But that clause 'nothing in India is identifiable' also hints at a property of the word 'nothing' which becomes vital to the meaning of the book.

'Nothing' as a word has two natures. Set alone it expresses stasis, vacancy: Nothing. As soon as it becomes part of a sentence, though, it makes the whole organisation of that sentence restless and unstable, expressive of contrary impulses. 'But nothing in India is identifiable.' On first reading, and predominantly always, this means, 'It is not possible to identify anything in India.' But there is another organisation lurking as a shadow form in that sentence, the possibility that 'Only in India is Nothing identifiable.' The suggestion here is faint. Take, however, Aziz's description of Akbar's religion, which sought to marry Hinduism and Mohammadenism and failed: 'Nothing embraces the whole of India, nothing, nothing . . .' (xiv, 156). The diagram of meaning is unstable, like an optical illusion. It alternates between 'There is nothing that embraces the whole of India' and – particularly with the force of the reiterated 'nothing' – 'Nothingness embraces the whole of India.' When the caves are described before the characters visit them (and previous to that passage commenting on Akbar's religion) the reader is told,

> Having seen one such cave, having seen two, having seen three, four, fourteen, twenty-four, the visitor returns to

Chandrapore uncertain whether he has had an interesting experience or a dull one or any experience at all. He finds it difficult to discuss the caves, or to keep them apart in his mind, for the pattern never varies, and no carving, not even a bees'-nest or a bat distinguishes one from another. Nothing, nothing attaches to them, and their reputation – for they have one – does not depend upon human speech.

(xii, 138)

We are entering the unsayable when we enter the caves: this is first expressed as alternation ('an interesting experience or a dull one') ending in negativity ('or any experience at all'). Identification and discrimination cannot be sustained (it's 'difficult to discuss the caves, or to keep them apart in his mind'). 'Nothing, nothing attaches to them.' In this instance 'Nothingness' begins to predominate in the sense over 'There is nothing that attaches to them'. 'Nothing' is a concept which is beyond human speech but which manifests itself as forceful. 'Nothing is inside them, they were sealed up before the creation of pestilence or treasure; if mankind grew curious and ex- cavated, nothing, nothing would be added to the sum of good or evil.' 'Nothing' diminishes again but does not revert to absence.

Nothing is concave and convex: it retreats from us and emerges out and confronts us. It alternates. Linguistically it subverts fixed orders, and produces echoes and disturbances of received meaning. Mrs Moore's experience in the cave is hideous because it challenges her values of individualism, discrimination and Christianity. The 'vile naked thing' which 'settled on her mouth like a pad' proves to have been 'a poor little baby, astride its mother's hip'. That knowledge cannot restore to her the language of Christianity, 'poor little talkative Christianity', because the echo has murmured: 'Everything exists, nothing has value' (xiv, 160). For her, and for us at this point in the book, that statement seems obliterative merely. But by the end of the book we are brought to see also that Nothing *has* value.

I want to look now at the ways in which this realisation comes about. Many of these ways are ways of negation and rejection, rather than of connection. Indeed 'Only connect', often taken as being apt for the whole of Forster's oeuvre rather than apposite only to *Howard's End*, is in this novel presented as insufficient and dangerous advice. It leads to bridge parties, false engagements, disastrous picnics. Dignity is reserved to separateness and absence: Aziz's dead wife, Mrs Moore's power at the trial in her absence and her celebration as Esmiss Esmoor, the absent Stella, Fielding's wife at the end of the book, Mrs Moore's daughter, whom we never directly meet; she is always described, always in the *other* boat – and the absence from the narrative of Aziz after his arrest until the trial is over. Early in the novel, at the end of chapter vii, Godbole explains the raga he has just sung:

> I placed myself in the position of a milkmaiden. I say to Shri Krishna, 'Come! Come to me only.' The God refuses to come. I grow humble and say; 'Do not come to me only. Multiply yourself into a hundred Krishnas, and let one go to each of my hundred companions, but one, O Lord of the Universe, come to me.' He refuses to come. This is repeated several times. . . .
>   'But He comes in some other song, I hope?' said Mrs Moore gently.
>   'Oh no, He refuses to come,' repeated Godbole, perhaps not understanding her question. 'I say to Him, Come, come, come, come, come, come. He neglects to come.'
>   Ronny's steps had died away, and there was a moment of absolute silence. No ripple disturbed the water, no leaf stirred.   (p. 96)

Absence is a condition of God as it is of nothingness, but equally, as Godbole explains a hundred pages later, 'Yet absence implies presence, absence is not non-existence' (xix, 186). Absence is pure, complete. Presence is skeined out in time. Rarely, and then only in moments recognised as ravishing, can the totality of a person be present. In absence, the whole may be realised, though realised as gone. For this reason desire and absence are interlocked: absolutes capable of expression only in negative form. In this book both of them find a place – a location – in the caves. Adela enters the caves thinking of the absent Ronny but not as an object of desire – on the contrary, she has just realised, 'She and Ronny – no, they did not love each other. . . . she felt like a mountaineer whose rope had broken. Not to love the man one's going to marry! Not to find it out till this moment! Not even to have asked oneself the question until now!' (xv, 163). She thinks about Aziz's sexual attractiveness, though 'she did not admire him with any personal warmth', and 'went into a cave, thinking with half her mind "sight-seeing bores me", and wondering with the other half about marriage'.

The entry into the caves and the descriptions of them have a sexual meaning which Forster recognises and develops. The caves which can be visited have been broached by man: 'elsewhere, deeper in the granite, are there certain chambers that have no entrances?. . . Local report declares that these exceed in number those that can be visited' (xii, 139). When a match is struck in the cave,

> two flames approach and strive to unite, but cannot, because one of them breathes air, the other stone. A mirror inlaid with lovely colours divides the lovers. . . . Fists and fingers thrust above the advancing soil – here at last is their skin, finer than any covering acquired by the animals, smoother than windless water, more voluptuous than love. The radiance increases, the flames touch one another, kiss, expire. The cave is dark again, like all the caves.   (pp. 138–9)

This language of desire and consummation is that of the flame and *its own reflection* – a reflexive place in which self divides into self and other, or, for Mrs Moore, the distinction between self and other can no longer be discriminatingly felt. These caves with their womb-like enclosure are not only representative of the female, but also figure a dread of the female and a vengeance taken on her. It is the women who suffer in them, impacted within their own symbol. Women's psychosexual experience, Lacan suggests, forms the blind spot within Freud's symbolic system. Forster, from his privileged sexually-ambiguous place, images a blind spot in the caves.

The image of perfection associated with the caves is of the Kawa Dol: 'the boulder that swings on the summit of the highest of the hills; a bubble-shaped cave that has neither ceiling nor floor, and mirrors its own darkness in every direction infinitely. If the boulder falls and smashes, the cave will smash too – empty as an Easter egg' (p. 139). The Kawa Dol is the perfection of enclosure: chaste nothingness mirroring its own darkness. In

contrast, we have the whimsical yet menacing language of
gestation and entry as Aziz searches fruitlessly for Adela
Quested, having lost her among the caves: 'Caves appeared in
every direction – it seemed their original spawning place – and
the orifices were always the same size' (xvi, 165).

The anthropomorphic or animistic, in which human forms
and human emotions are used to express the non-human, is
employed by Forster in this novel, but it always takes a disrupted
or disruptive form. At the end of the first chapter comes the first
reference to 'the prostrate earth' which 'lies flat, heaves a little,
is flat again. Only in the south, where a group of fists and fingers
are thrust up through the soil, is the endless expanse
interrupted' (i, 32). The suggested image of the human body is
violated, interrupted, by the grotesqueness of 'a group of fists
and fingers thrust up through the soil', and the geological
description that opens 'Caves' (again cast in many negatives)
culminates in a disturbingly tactile passage to describe the
immeasurable age and dryness of 'the high places of Dravidia':

> No water has ever covered them, and the sun who has
> watched them for countless aeons may still discern in their
> outlines forms that were his before our globe was torn from
> his bosom. If flesh of the sun's flesh is to be touched
> anywhere, it is here, among the incredible antiquity of these
> hills.   (xii, 137)

The usual function of anthropomorphism is to domesticate the
non-human into meaning, an activity which reinstates man at
the centre. Forster in his book constantly reminds us of the other
inhabitants of India: the animals, the plants, the birds, the
stones – particularly the stones. In the caves the human becomes
simply another substance, 'a naked pad'; and the evening after
the catastrophe Fielding, in a paranoid moment, 'saw the fists
and fingers of the Marabar swell until they included the whole
night sky'. The powers of the human mind and the attempt to
perceive all other elements of life in terms of the human creates
claustrophobia and oppression. So at the beginning of the book
the Christian missionaries argue about how far the mercy of God
may extend: 'And the wasps? He became uneasy during the
descent to wasps, and was apt to change the conversation. And
oranges, cactuses, crystals and mud? And the bacteria inside Mr

Sorley? No, no, this is going too far. We must exclude someone from our gathering, or we shall be left with nothing' (iv, 58).

On this return to that sentence it becomes clearer that *'everything exists'* and that 'nothing *has* value'. Mrs Moore can reach and recognise the wasp in her love – 'Pretty thing'; Godbole dancing his religious dance at the end can recognise Mrs Moore and the wasp:

> Chance brought her into his mind while it was in this heated state, he did not select her, she happened to occur among the throng of soliciting images, a tiny splinter, and he impelled her by his spiritual force to that place where completeness can be found. Completeness, not reconstruction. His senses grew thinner, he remembered a wasp seen he forgot where, perhaps on a stone. He loved the wasp equally, he impelled it likewise, he was imitating God. And the stone where the wasp clung – could he . . . no, he could not, he had been wrong to attempt the stone, logic and conscious effort had seduced. . . .   (xxxiii, 283–4)

Although Godbole is moving towards completeness not hierarchy, he also balks at the stone. The stones are obdurate matter, and will not yield to human meaning; just as the sky's space will not permit any conclusion, which would accommodate it to human perception. Extension and matter both challenge meaning, are part of that negativity which is the fullness beyond the human. Nothingness may equally be full or empty, absence or completeness.

In the earlier two books, 'Mosque' and 'Caves', alternation and pairing are tested as ways of encompassing meaning. 'Either–or' sentences are extremely frequent; early on Aziz says of the English, 'Why be either friends with the fellows or not friends?' (ii, 35). 'To be or not to be married, that was the question, and they had decided it in the affirmative' (viii, 109) – a formulation whose abstractedness suggests rather a bleak, diminished negation.

Alternation is neither dualism nor dialectic. In Hegelian dialectic two negations thrust through towards a positive outcome. In this book, there is rather a sense of prolongation, attenuation and loss connected with alternation and with the attempt to stabilise it by pairing. It is a way of using negativity

which deprives it of its latent positive force and makes it function
as that which mists, blurs, stains, tarnishes, spreads too thin.
This form of negation permits no escape into energy. The wisest
course in this text is to resist the obvious way out of alternation:
that of pairing. Adela and Fielding shake hands like two dwarfs
but eschew all other attempts to make arches. The two great
props to marriage, we are later told, are religion and society.
But neither of them is marriage. The crown to that arch is
missing. The idea of pairing is absurdly, linguistically, reduced
in the figure of the clergyman who accompanies Adela on an
expedition from the ship on her way home. ' "He turns to the
East, he *re*turns to the West." . . . The missionary looked at her
humorously, in order to cover the emptiness of his mind. He had
no idea what he meant by "turn" and "return", but he often
used words in pairs, for the sake of moral brightness' (xxix,
263).

A better possibility is posed in the refreshed nominalism of
Mrs Moore, leaving India. The train passes 'a place called
Asirgarh which she passed at sunset and identified on a map'.

> No one had ever mentioned Asirgarh to her, but it had huge
> and noble bastions and to the right of them was a mosque. She
> forgot it. Ten minutes later, Asirgarh reappeared. The
> mosque was to the left of the bastions now. The train in its
> descent through the Vindyas had described a semicircle
> round Asirgarh. *What could she connect it with except its own
> name? Nothing; she knew no-one who lived there.* But it had
> looked at her twice and seemed to say: *'I do not vanish.'*
> (xxiii, 213; emphasis added)

Mrs Moore accepts lack of connection, semi-circularity,
inversion, absence, the place 'not in terms of her own trouble'.

After the defining negative of Adela's answer in the
courtroom, moving from 'I am not quite sure', through shaking
her head, to 'No', new possibilities of meaning beginning to
emerge. Indeterminacy is not abolished, however: we never
know what happened in the caves, who followed her or whether
anyone followed her – and to prove a man's innocence is to
prove his non-involvement. Innocence moreover is there
already and should need no proof. The act of proof creates
nothing fresh.

The dreaming beauty and impassivity of the naked punkah wallah, his absolute *inattention* to the proceedings of the court as he pulls the fan, has released Adela. She has looked at what needs no interpretation or rationalisation. She is released from the need to identify. The detective-story level of the plot has seemed to insist upon the importance of identification, but such efforts of the will and of the positive prove meagre. Only identification *with* has worth; identification *of* is paltry. That is why negation is the form that truth must take. So the holy and infuriating Godbole refuses directly to answer the question, 'Is Aziz innocent or guilty?' put to him by Fielding, saying only that 'nothing can be performed in isolation. All perform a good action, when one is performed, and when an evil action is performed, all perform it' (xix, 185).

At the beginning of 'Temple', alternation poises itself upon positive meaning. God 'is, was not, is not, was'. In this book attributes may be lost without loss of significance. The titles of all three books suggest enclosure: 'Mosque', 'Caves' and 'Temple'. But in this last book almost everything happens outdoors. There is a sense of free exteriority – water, boats on the tank, the festival happening everywhere. Very early on in the text we were told that no Indian animal has any sense of an interior. In this final book there is no need to exclude anyone or anything from the gathering. Not everyone understands the events, but they are all there, milling around. Discrimination is lost: when the villagers glimpse the image 'a most beautiful and radiant expression came into their faces, a beauty in which there was nothing personal, for it caused them all to resemble one another during the moment of its indwelling, and only when it was withdrawn did they revert to individual clods' (xxxiii, 281–2). 'Imitations' and 'substitutions' 'awake in each man according to his capacity, an emotion he could not have had otherwise. No definite image survived; at the Birth it was questionable whether a silver doll, or a mud village, or a silk napkin, or an intangible spirit, or a pious resolution, had been born' (p. 287). 'The choir was repeating and inverting the names of deities.' 'God si love.' These possibilities are all imitations of each other and momentary representations of a truth which does not require to be said. The whole festival is in honour of *the God without attributes*.

So, attributelessness, which in the caves had been

claustrophobic and annihilating, here becomes playful and spacious. We are told that when Aziz came to this state of Mau he had pleased people by stating at his inauguration '*I study nothing. I respect*' (xxxiv, 289; emphasis added). By this point in the process of the text, the reader recognises the completeness suggested by the word 'nothing'. Negatives can be used lightheartedly. In the final chapter Aziz and Fielding ride together, argue, discuss 'as if nothing had happened' and a cobra crawls across a grassy slope bright with butterflies 'doing nothing in particular, and disappeared among some custard apple trees' (xxxvii, 311).

In the final paragraph, which I quoted at the beginning, separateness and equality are emphasised. The two riders swerve together and apart. They must ride single file, surrounded by the animate and inanimate other beings of India: horses, earth, rocks, temples, tank, jail, palace, birds, carrion, Guest House: 'they didn't want it, they said in their hundred voices, "No, not yet", and the sky said, "No, not there." '

'In space things touch, in time they part.' Narrative always sets things in sequence. So throughout this work negation and 'nothing' are active rather than static, because they are energised by being involved in sentences, in paragraphs, in chapters. Their meaning is to some extent controlled by their being part of narration, rather than, say, of a lyric poem. But the uses of negation, alternation, and the indeterminate make it possible for the text to register that which is not to be said, not to be written (as within the book Aziz never writes the poem he plans, whose topic constantly changes).

In the *Bhagavad-Gita* it is said that God may be defined only by negatives. Forster's novel challenges through the habitual negativity of its language the beleaguered humanism of its characters. Forster's work presages the end of Empire, not simply the end of the Raj in India (though it does that), but also the end of that struggle for dominion which is implicit in the struggle for language and meaning – the struggle to keep man at the centre of the universe. He sees that what lies beyond the human need not be null or void. But it was not the readers of the 1920s who saw it thus: it is we sixty years later who can recognise this 'pressentiment collectif, projet, aspiration'. And we can do so by studying not what is absent, but what is there: the language of the text.

5 Listening to Language

JUDITH SCHERER HERZ

Language is at once the subject of *A Passage to India*, its intractable medium, its clarifying agency, and its astounding, if finally hapless, accomplishment. As the narrator uses it, its resources are multiple, for there is always another discrimination to be made, another nuance to be discovered. But as his characters use it, language is often enfeebled or dislocated: for the British it is a sign system adrift from its signifieds; for the Indians, a sign system pointing only to other signs. Even those who strive for silence – Godbole or Mrs Moore, for example – hear the noise that is *in* the silence not as an alternative but, especially for Mrs Moore, as yet another terrifying and unknown tongue. There are words, there are things, there is noise, there is silence. On these four co-ordinates Forster constructs a pattern that, far more than the plot of marriage, colonisation and friendship, provides the novel with its narrative power.

We are not, however, simply passive witnesses to that power, for, more than any of his other novels, *A Passage to India* trains our ears, forces us to listen acutely, teaches us to discriminate sounds, words, voices. Furthermore, by having his characters listen to each other, by listening to them carefully himself, Forster makes the process of choosing and testing language an act of enormous consequence. We hear the characters' speech and the justifications and evasions behind the speech. By this double process of speaking and listening, Forster is able to explore the language of his own fiction, making that language itself a crucial part of the novel's subject.[1] As a result the reader is made extraordinarily attentive, since he is forced to supplement the narrator's discriminations with his own.

It is a complex process. A character speaks, another character

narrator hears them both, and embeds their speech –
̇d subtext – in his narration, which we hear directly as
auditors and receive indirectly as mediated readers.[2] Two
paragraphs early in the novel illustrate this clearly.

> He spoke sincerely. Every day he worked hard in the court
> trying to decide which of two untrue accounts was the less
> untrue, trying to dispense justice fearlessly, to protect the
> weak against the less weak, the incoherent against the
> plausible, surrounded by lies and flattery. That morning he
> had convicted a railway clerk of overcharging pilgrims for
> their tickets, and a Pathan of attempted rape. He expected no
> gratitude, no recognition for this, and both clerk and Pathan
> might appeal, bribe their witnesses more effectually in the
> interval, and get their sentences reversed. It was his duty. But
> he did expect sympathy from his own people, and except from
> newcomers he obtained it. He did think he ought not to be
> worried about Bridge Parties when the day's work was over
> and he wanted to play tennis with his equals or rest his legs
> upon a long chair.
>
> He spoke sincerely, but she could have wished with less
> gusto. How Ronny revelled in the drawbacks of his situation!
> How he did rub it in that he was not in India to behave
> pleasantly, and derived positive satisfaction therefrom! He
> reminded her of his public-school days. The traces of
> young-man humanitarianism had sloughed off, and he talked
> like an intelligent and embittered boy. His words without his
> voice might have impressed her, but when she heard the
> self-satisfied lilt of them, when she saw the mouth moving so
> complacently and competently beneath the little red nose, she
> felt, quite illogically, that this was not the last word on India.
> One touch of regret – not the canny substitute but the true
> regret from the heart – would have made him a different man,
> and the British Empire a different institution.   (v, 69–70)

These two interior paragraphs occur simultaneously with a
preceding paragraph of direct speech. There Ronny has been
justifying his new Anglo-Indian sensibility to his mother: 'We're
not pleasant in India, and we don't intend to be pleasant. We've
something more important to do' (p. 69). The third-person
point of view is used to suggest a first-person meditation, a silent

speech behind the quoted speech, as if Ronny were thinking through his words at the same time as he was speaking them. The sincerity that the narrator credits him with is not so much contradicted over the course of the paragraph as rendered irrelevant. The terms of the justification ('to decide which of two untrue accounts was the less untrue') collide awkwardly with the myth of the Sahib ('to dispense justice fearlessly') and then dwindle meekly down to 'his duty'. And by a simple shift in the form of the past tense ('he worked', 'he expected', to 'he *did* expect', 'he *did* think') the underlying petulance of the implied speaker is clearly heard. As Forster paraphrases Ronny's situation totally from Ronny's perspective, we understand that, from the point of view of officialdom, this 'duty' consists of details only; there is no design and thus no possible 'bridge party'. The final image has a lovely two-way thrust. Ronny indeed might have used these very words, totally unaware of the way in which they caricature the ruler safe in his enclave, with his tennis, his 'equals' and his legs upon a long chair.

In the first paragraph the narrator is listening to a character think; in the second he is observing that process at one remove, and, as Mrs Moore listens to her son, it is the voice that she pays attention to more than the words. This time the statement of sincerity is immediately qualified: sincerity is defined as self-satisfaction, duty as mere complacency. She intuits the discrepancy between man and task by hearing the difference between voice and words, a distinction that Forster emphasises by this double framing of a single statement, the first paragraph examining the words, the second the voice. If for Mrs Moore, as for most of the Indian characters, the heart must inform the tongue, then the very way that Ronny speaks cancels out the supposed sincerity of his words. His mouth moves mechanically; mouth and nose seem to have no organic connection. Thus in much the same way that the catalogue of self-justifications in the first paragraph becomes, from the narrator's shaping point of view, an indictment of both the man and the task, so the observations of Mrs Moore become transformed by the narrator into a revalued image of the meaning of Empire. (She observes the absence of regret; he enlarges that observation into a generalisation that the entire narrative will support and examine.) Both paragraphs begin and end similarly, but from the vantage of the close of the second, tennis and long chairs become even more emphatically elements of a debased, even dangerous, version of Empire.

As readers we should do well to follow Mrs Moore's lead and listen to the voice inside the language, particularly in a fiction where language is in large measure the subject. And India, source of all our Western languages, is entirely apposite as a setting for such an enterprise. It is an India, however, that is mediated by Whitman's myth-and-language-making. For Whitman's poem 'Passage to India', from which Forster took his title, is, like the novel, a meditation on the beginnings of language – 'the myths Asiatique, the primitive fables', 'the retrospect brought forward' into the poem's new time, new language, new continent:

> Europe to Asia, Africa join'd, and they to the New World
> The lands, geographies, dancing before you, holding a festival garland,
> As brides and bridegrooms hand in hand.[3]

Whitman's vast optimism, however, was not Forster's, for in the novel the wedding of East and West is, at the very least, postponed for another time, another place. None the less he used the Whitmanic metaphor to explore tentatively and ironically the possibilities of 'bridging', of constructing a common speech, a shared idiom.

But prior to all language there is the sound that echoes in the caves, the sterile syllable that constantly divides into itself – 'boum' or 'ou boum' or 'bou-oum' – a sound that excludes meaning, that undermines all structures built from words. It is an empty sound, fit creation of the 'hollow egg', the Kawa Dol, 'original spawning place of all the caves'. Indeed, in these terms the description of the caves is an extraordinary *tour de force*, for language has to be pushed beyond its own resources. The caves are presented as outside the range of language, as 'unspeakable', as not dependent 'upon human speech'. Even to locate them in time, Forster has to set up a sequence that goes back before beginnings so that 'immemorial' becomes recent, measurable in historic time. This going-back becomes a process of shedding, of renunciation, ending finally in inarticulateness:

Nothing, nothing attaches to them, and their reputation – for they have one – does not depend upon human speech. It is as if the surrounding plain or the passing birds have taken upon themselves to exclaim 'Extraordinary!' and the word has taken root in the air. . . . (xii, 138)

Inarticulateness is thus both the source of language and its antithesis, just as speech in the novel is now meaningless noise, now a hard-won victory over chaos and disorder. And there is always the danger of 'the inarticulate world . . . [resuming] control as soon as men are tired' (x, 126). This observation forms the centre of the chapter linking the two halves of Aziz's sick-bed conversation. It is a chapter that reduces landscape to alien noise and the glare of a sinister sun. The very air prevents language from forming. Space is filled first with noise – the squeaks of the squirrels, the creaking of the brown birds – and then with something less defined but more oppressively felt: 'The space between them . . . instead of being empty, was clogged with a medium that pressed against their flesh' (x, 126).[4] Inside as well there is an oppressive quality. Language is full of noise, of misunderstanding and innuendo. As the 'comforters' gather around his bed, using words to parry, manipulate, signal and incite, Aziz retreats into his quilt, providing a comically accurate visual image for a form of speech that works against connection and communication.[5] The false suggestion of Godbole's supposed cholera, for example, prompts several outbursts from those in attendance. Mr Syed Mohammed 'in his excitement . . . fell into Punjabi (he came from that side) and was unintelligible' (ix, 118). It is a comic detail certainly. It has the effect of making the reader hear a language that he does not know. But it also emphasises the idea of language as a means of separation or division, the verbal analogue of Aziz wrapped in his quilt. And appropriately Aziz emerges from his quilt when he begins to speak the language that will temporarily at least produce the 'feeling that India was one' (p. 119). The poetry he speaks cancels divisiveness not for what the words say but for the feeling they communicate in the 'indifferent air'. The words work because of certain agreed-upon conventions, conventions which reduce language to a set of ritual gestures. The listeners are overwhelmed by the poem's pathos but they are certainly not attending to the words. The Police Inspector, for example, 'sat with his mind empty, and when his thoughts, which were mainly ignoble, flowed back into it, they had a pleasant freshness'. Language operates here on the level of sound. But the unity that it invokes is both spurious and fleeting; it lasts only 'until they looked out of the door' (ibid.).

This substitution of feeling for meaning is presented as the primary characteristic of Indian speech.[6] Words are viewed as a musical notation that carries the feeling which *is* the true meaning. So soon as the music ceases to sound, poetry becomes prose and the statement is no longer true. As Aziz recited Ghalib he believed for the moment that 'India was one'. Later, however, when Adela says almost the same thing – she is looking for something that will 'embrace the whole of India' – Aziz replies almost angrily, 'Nothing embraces the whole of India', for so soon as his dream of 'universal brotherhood . . . was put into prose it became untrue' (xiv, 156).

Since language encompasses both prose and poetry, it is perhaps an oversimplification to say as John Colmer does that language divides, silence unites.[7] Language is potentially divisive, certainly, but it is also the chief means of staving off the anarchy of the inarticulate world. It stands opposed to noise as much as to silence, and silence, too, may be ominous. The silence that follows Godbole's song of the Lord of the Universe who refuses to come offers no comfort whatsoever. It is as baffling and unavailing as the unintelligible noises of his song and is the visible proof of the absence of divinity: 'No ripple disturbed the water, no leaf stirred' (vii, 96).[8] There are several other moments of silence in the novel, few of them comforting. The silence that accompanies the procession to the caves caused everything to seem 'cut off at its root, and therefore infected with illusion' (xiv, 152).

If there is any unity to be found, and Forster seems to doubt this even as he intensifies the search, it will not be in silence but in a language that will, in the words of *Howards End* (xxii, 183–4), connect the passion and the prose. As Fielding and Aziz part at the end of 'Caves', a union in separation that adumbrates the final parting, they discuss poetry. The topic is proposed as something innocuous, something that will deflect their attention from what was happening beneath their words. But it suddenly enlarges: 'I like this conversation', says Aziz. 'It may lead to something interesting' (xxxi, 273). The something it leads to is Fielding's perception that language must aspire to a state of music. Whatever the Hindus have found in religion, he observes, they have not been able to transform to song. That is why he had hoped that Aziz would continue writing religious poetry. The result would not necessarily have been true, but it none the less needed to have been sung. From this point of view the song of Godbole is something prior to language. It is a maze of noises, the song of an unknown bird. Or that is how it is heard by the Western ear, perhaps even by the Moslem ear.

But, in turn, the speech of the British, for all its precision and accuracy, is not necessarily intelligible to the Indians. What perplexed them most about Fielding's speech was its trust in language for itself. His words were 'too definite and bleak. Unless a sentence paid a few compliments to Justice and Morality in passing, its grammar wounded their ears and paralysed their minds' (ix, 125). Fielding is a polite listener in this scene, but his words and theirs never seem to connect. Whereas he is busy trying to catch their words, the Indians are simply pleased by his presence.

In the original version, as Fielding listened to Aziz praising the unattractive Rafi, he had the sense that 'something had gone before he didn't understand'.[9] Earlier, at Fielding's tea party, when Aziz had attempted to lead Godbole into revealing something about the caves, there was played out a similar drama of the separation of words from their meaning. Aziz realised that Godbole 'was keeping back something about the caves'; not intentionally, but his mind had none the less been silenced. Adela, who had been following closely every word of the conversation, was unaware that she had missed it entirely: 'The dialogue remained light and friendly, and Adela had no conception of its underdrift' (vii, 92).

This underdrift, a mode of speech in which the words that constitute conversation are only tenuously connected to a deeper layer, is a significant feature of Indian speech. Much of Forster's most interesting exploration of the nature of language takes place in this linguistic space. It is the meeting-ground between listener and speaker; it is the space where the disruptions and discontinuities caused by language occur and where a new link between speaker and hearer can be forged. It is involved as well with Fielding's notion that part of language is song.

The separation of words and meaning takes other forms as

well. In a frequently recurring pattern, a split is certainly present, but as little is going on beneath the surface as is being carried by the words themselves. The Nawab Bahadur's 'oration' is a good example. Relegated to the front seat by Miss Derek after her first successful 'rescue party' on the Marabar Road, 'he grew more and more voluble'. His words, however, had no content in themselves; rather they expressed an elaborate social pattern: to endorse Miss Quested's remark but not so as to diminish his own social bigness, certainly not to let her think she had committed a discourtesy and so on. He knew his audience felt no interest, indeed was not even listening, but it did not matter: 'his life . . . ran on as before and expressed itself in streams of well-chosen words' (viii, 108).

Sometimes words carry *only* their meaning and the pathos of such scenes is a result of the characters' being unable to give them resonance or echo. Adela in the episode of the non-naming of the unknown bird and the accident with the unnamed animal, decides that she and Ronny need a 'thorough talk'. But their words are impoverished; very few of them suffice for the little they have to say. Adela wants to make this scene of the breaking of the not yet acknowledged engagement into something more. But the silence, largely a function of Ronny's taciturnity ('I don't much believe in this discussing' – p. 99), limits them. There is a quality of pantomime to the scene as if they were dwarfed by the awareness that the scene should have been bigger.

Such a quality is explicitly observed in a later scene when, after the trial, Adela and Fielding discover themselves having just such 'thorough talks'. They use words carefully; neither of them seeks Ronny's evasion of silence. They share common assumptions and, gradually, over the course of their 'curious conversations', even subscribe to the same statements. Their words are not entirely lacking in underdrift, but they do not know how to operate together in such a space. They feel remote as if they can barely see the paucity of their gestures, hence the marvellous metaphor of dwarfs shaking hands. That they are aware of this gives the scene its wistfulness, but, although they 'spoke the same language', there seems to be an enormous gap between its tiny sound and the universe in which those sounds echo.

In these last two examples, language may fail, but its

practitioners try to make it serve the truth as they have come to understand it. But language may be treacherous as well, and not simply in the malicious, gossipy sense of the sick-room conversation where haemorrhoids turn into cholera and the dark suspicion of political plots. The impetus to the expedition that no one wanted, for example, is an overheard conversation. The conversation itself, like the Nawab Bahadur's oration, had no meaning. It was language as time-filler, a social response prompted by a picturesque and distant scene. But the words become falsely fixed; they are assigned meaning: the ladies were offended, they had expected an invitation daily. Thus nothing becomes a false something in much the same way as the caves themselves take on history and meaning despite their emptiness, in much the same way as the Kawa Dol, the empty egg, takes on the history of the event that didn't happen, the event without a name, in much the same way as the 'withered and twisted stump of a toddy-palm' (xiv, 152) becomes a venomous black cobra. Once words take root in the air, they grow with surprising tenacity.

From one point of view the novel suggests that the process of fixing experience in language, of naming, is simple, but from another this same process is seen as enormously difficult. Although the false word may take ready root in the air, there are times when one has no word at all. Some experience, some animal, some bird always remains outside one's power to name: 'Nothing in India is identifiable, the mere asking of a question causes it to disappear or to merge in something else' (viii, 101). Adela and Ronny cannot name the animal that attacked the car, they cannot name the bird; Adela cannot name her assailant or even name her experience. And just when the novel is most concerned with naming, when every reader wants to know, on the simplest level of story-telling, what happened, Forster comically swerves away from the issue and has Godbole inquire of Fielding what name he should give his new school, his insistence on naming all the more remarkable for his refusal to say whether or not a catastrophe had occurred, whether or not Aziz was guilty.

As readers we may well share Fielding's exasperation with Godbole, but Godbole's response is not as absurd as it is often taken to be. Given the dangers of language as we have observed them, one must proceed cautiously with (or channel harmlessly into the naming of a school that within a year become a granary) the impulse to fix, to name. After all, Adela at the trial finally says no more than Godbole had. She simply 'failed to locate him' (xxiv, 231) and as a result, she was 'not quite sure'. All through the scene she was exceptionally careful of her words, each syllable of even the most trivial statements ('I'll thank you this evening') carefully formed 'as if her trouble would diminish if it were accurately defined' (p. 216). But definition eludes her as well.

Closely related to naming, but essentially antithetical to it, is labelling. It is seen as a process of diminishing language, whereas naming may enlarge it. Adela fears that by marrying Ronny she will 'become what is known as an Anglo-Indian . . . it's inevitable. I can't avoid the label' (xiv, 157). Fielding knows that by supporting Aziz he will be called 'anti-British', 'seditious'. He had hoped 'to slink through India unlabelled' (xix, 183). Labelling falsifies the relationship between the word and the thing signified; it arrests what is a fluid and constantly changing relationship. When Adela finds herself, after the incident with the Nawab Bahadur, suddenly engaged to be married, she discovers that 'she was labelled now', and the immediate consequence of this is that there is no longer room for talk, not even for the ghostly 'thorough talk' that was to have signalled the end of their relationship. The narrator remarks, 'what indeed is there to say?' (viii, 109). Labelling reduces language to a rigid code. At the arrest the Collector is most enraged that Fielding does not respond automatically to the label 'an English girl fresh from England' (xvii, 174). The Nawab Bahadur speaks similarly: he will not let 'an innocent Moslem perish' (xxiv, 217). These are both in fact true statements. What falsifies them is that they are being used as labels, to obscure rather than to make distinctions. What Adela does at the trial is, as we have seen, exactly the opposite. She must make herself distinguish exactly what had occurred. Ironically, the more she does this, the less interesting she becomes to the other British, who had turned her, the 'English girl fresh from England', into a symbol, a label of their relationship with India.

One feels in all Forster's writing the primacy of the word. The idea, the statement, grows out of the implications of the word; it follows the logic of the metaphor.[10] Failure to perceive this has led to some crucial misreadings: a particularly notable one, F. R. Leavis's, deserves some scrutiny. Leavis quotes the passage where Hamidullah and Fielding tacitly acknowledge their inability to grieve at the news of Mrs Moore's death:

> How indeed is it possible for one human being to be sorry for all the sadness that meets him on the face of the earth, for the pain that is endured not only by men, but by animals and plants, and perhaps by the stones? (xxvi, 247).

Leavis finds the word 'stones' a remarkable 'lapse': 'Can one do anything but reflect how extraordinary it is that so fine a writer should be able in such a place, to be so little certain just how serious he is.'[11] He implies that the inclusion of the word is mere whimsy, an example of Forster's not being able to resist the *reductio ad absurdum*. In fact, however, that word is the validation of a statement made two pages earlier to explain Hamidullah's inability to understand Adela's honesty and sense of justice. To the Indian these were not enough without an unstinting love, 'unless the word that was with God also is God' (p. 245). But if all that is is of God, then all that is can both participate in that joy and suffer pain. There can be no exclusion, not even stones. That the 'advanced' Mr Sorley becomes uneasy at the wasps and would exclude crystals, mud and bacteria from the scheme of salvation is by no means the book's statement. And in the catalogue of universal gradations, stones occupy the same position as crystal and mud. Fielding and Hamidullah, in their momentary contact over the possibility of shared grief, like Mr Graysford and Mr Sorley, also draw the line. They do it, however, with more self-knowledge, a more determined desire to hold on to the little they do understand.

Once a word has been given a place in the fiction, it continues to resound. Stones and rocks remain part of the novel's language, registering the joy and the sorrow, to the very last action. That last ride begins amid 'jolly bushes and rocks'; the friends are together; 'the Marabar is wiped out'. But by the end of the scene the jolly rocks quite literally enforce the separation, the earth 'sending up rocks through which the riders must pass single file' (the verb an ominous reminder of the first description of the caves, where the 'fists and fingers are thrust up through the soil' – i, 32). The catalogue syntax enacts the idea as well.

The effect is linear; the nouns proceed single-file. But counterbalancing this is the rhythmically dominant pairing of 'and then', 'and then', which sets up another metrical pattern with 'no not yet' and 'no not there'. The coupling of the phrases contrasts with the discreet procession of the nouns. Syntactically there is both union and separation, inclusion and exclusion. The qualified negation 'not *yet*' is thus confirmed as temporary by its proposed completion, 'and then'.

To be sure this last sentence has had as many interpretations as there are readings of the novel. But however one finally interprets it, one must first listen to it, feel its rhythms, examine its words. Not one word has arrived in it untested. All have been explored throughout the fiction and have earned their place in this final, albeit paradoxical, description of a landscape rendered audible, a landscape that requires careful listening as well as accurate vision. And what is true for this last sentence is, in varying degrees, true for all the sentences in the novel. Reading it requires that we attend closely to language, to voice, to all of the words, even to the stones. Thus, while language in *A Passage to India* is challenged by its own demonstrated insufficiency, it also constitutes the means of that demonstration. Language is offered paradoxically as the text's ultimate achievement even as it is undermined in its unfolding by a structure of mutually excluding discourses. If language is sometimes made to seem little more than noise, it is (to borrow Forster's description of Beethoven's Fifth) 'sublime noise' indeed.

6   Muddle *et cetera*: Syntax in *A Passage to India*

MOLLY TINSLEY

> If we had to decide which of the legacies of Ancient Greece
> has meant more to Europe and mankind, we might well
> nominate the complex sentence. Along with Greek
> philosophy, there grew up a language able to express its fine
> distinctions and carefully ordered thought.[1]

It is with some notion of the connection between culture and
sentence structure that E. M. Forster begins his treatment of
Leonard Bast in *Howards End*. Leonard, bent on escaping the
abyss where no one counts, reads *Stones of Venice* assiduously,
memorising cadences and trying to adapt Ruskin's complex
structures to his own mediocre experience. But Leonard is just
sensitive enough to realise the inappropriateness of his efforts.
The glorious rhythms of Venice are not for him. He must stick to
simple sentences such as 'My flat is dark as well as stuffy'
(vi, 47). Oddly enough, Leonard Bast anticipates Forster's own
struggle later to develop sentences that would aptly reflect the
experience of India. He too had to leave behind the harmonies
of the Mediterranean, the 'spirit in a reasonable form', as
inappropriate to a muddled civilisation where 'everything was
placed wrong'. (*PI*, xxxii, 278) If, as Turner suggests, orderly
hypotaxis is a correlative for European civilisation, it is not
surprising to find the Forster of *A Passage to India* exploring
ways to discard or at least disrupt it.

In fact, the sentence that establishes itself in *A Passage to
India*, if not as the norm at least as a conspicuous motif, is a
loosely co-ordinated sequence that sputters along, refusing the
potential emphasis of parallelism, and falling into subordinate

71

structures not so much to clarify distinctions as to introduce tangential detail. Aziz's quest for the picnic elephant, for example, unwinds its syntax, finally illustrating the contingency of grand events on minutiae. Semi-official, this beast

> was best approached through the Nawab Bahadur, who was best approached through Nureddin, but he never answered letters, but his mother had great influence with him and he was a friend of Hamidullah Begum's, who had been excessively kind and had promised to call on her provided the broken shutter of the purdah carriage came back soon enough from Calcutta.   (xiv, 151)

Sentences such as this, muddled and lumpy as an Indian landscape, seem to have relinquished two conventions of Western form – climax and closure. In so doing, they enforce stylistically the issues at the heart of Forster's theme.

The details of Adela's assault comprise another loose amalgam of co-ordinate and subordinate structures:

> She had struck the polished wall – for no reason – and before the comment had died away, he followed her, and the climax was the falling of her field-glasses.   (xxii, 200)

This sentence contains its own ironic comment on climax: the potential for syntactic emphasis is thrown away on the second of the three co-ordinated elements, the left-brancher, while the assertion of climax in the third is undercut by its identification with 'falling', the cadence of 'field-glasses', and, of course, by its evasion of the sexual implication. There is a similar play on Western form in the recounting of the legend of the water tank:

> It concerned a Hindu Rajah who had slain his own sister's son, and the dagger with which he performed the deed remained clamped to his hand until in the course of years he came to the Marabar Hills, where he was thirsty and wanted to drink but saw a thirsty cow and ordered the water to be offered to her first, which, when done, 'dagger fell from his hand, and to commemorate miracle he built Tank'.   (xix, 186–7)

Godbole's conversations, we are then told, often 'culminated' in a cow. Certainly the disintegrating syntax of this single sentence mocks all notions of the culmination.

Anticlimax, of course, acquires thematic resonance in *A Passage to India*. The Indian sunrise, the picnic, the trial, the Hindu festival – all are its manifestations. It is the condition of the time-bound, fact-bound world which denies men the 'poetry' they 'yearn for', denies joy grace, sorrow augustness, and infinity form (xxiv, 215). It is what one is left with when 'God' has passed, and he is always passing. Thus, the dwindling festivities of the 'Temple' section:

> Some of the torches went out, fireworks didn't catch, there began to be less singing, and the tray returned to Professor Godbole, who picked up a fragment of the mud adhering and smeared it on his forehead without much ceremony   (xxxvi, 310)

Here the fluctuating imprecision of the clauses joins with Godbole's gesture of humility to mark the dissolution of vision.

Forster's sentences in *A Passage to India* fight closure as consistently as they undermine climax. Numerous final ellipses as well as three 'etc.'s violate the rhetoric of well-made sentences, and more than a dozen times in the course of the novel, Forster adds extra elements to his sentences by means of a simple, unsubtle 'also'. In many instances these afterthoughts represent the pressure of the lower 'inarticulate world' which in India 'is closer at hand and readier to resume control as soon as men are tired' (x, 126). Thus Adela lies passive in shock:

> She had been touched by the sun, also hundreds of cactus spines had to be picked out of her flesh.   (xxii, 199)

During the May festival, the inarticulate world is invited to encroach and be loved – 'birds, caves, railways, and the stars' (xxxiii, 285).

> A cobra of papier-mâché now appeared on the carpet, also a wooden cradle swinging from a frame.   (ibid.)

> [The Rajah] could witness the Three Steps by which the Saviour ascended the universe to the discomfiture of Indra,

also the death of the dragon, the mountain that turned into an umbrella, and the saddhu who (with comic results) invoked the God before dining.   (xxxvi, 299)

Snakes twist their way through the narrative of the novel as images of those lower pressures so dangerous to civilisation. It seems appropriate, then, that the cobra should take a final, casual bow at the parting of Aziz and Fielding, by means of an 'also':

> Presently the ground opened into full sunlight and they saw a grassy slope bright with butterflies, also a cobra, which crawled across doing nothing in particular . . .   (xxxvii, 311)

Along with the anticlimactic sentences, then, these additions seem to pay tribute to the ragged edges, the formlessness of the Indian experience. No sentence, in other words, is so sacred that it cannot be reopened and altered by the emergence of a new fact. In this Forster affirms stylistically that Hindu sense of heaven which so horrified the Western missionaries. 'And oranges, cactuses, crystals and mud? and the bacteria inside Mr Sorley?' – it was 'going too far' to include all these in their Lord's mansions. In an ironic comment that forecasts the exploded rhetoric of *A Passage to India*, the missionaries insist, 'We must exclude someone from our gathering or we shall be left with nothing' (iv, 58).

Perhaps the most recurring departure in *A Passage* from the refined logic of hypotaxis is the comma-spliced sentence. In certain cases, spliced co-ordination seems to evoke the rapid overlay of thought or action that approximates the jumble of simultaneity. The verdict is delivered, for instance:

> then the flimsy framework of the court broke up, the shouts of derision and rage culminated, people screamed and cursed, kissed one another, wept passionately.   (xxiv, 232)

Interestingly enough, these run-on sentences are expressive not only of chaos but also of ecstasy. Thus Godbole achieves his limited communion with the Other:

> Chance brought her [Mrs Moore] into his mind while it was in

this heated state, he did not select her, she happened to occur among the throng of soliciting images, a tiny splinter, and he impelled her by his spiritual force to that place where completeness can be found. . . . His senses grew thinner, he remembered a wasp seen he forgot where, perhaps on a stone. He loved the wasp equally, he impelled it likewise, he was imitating God. And the stone where the wasp clung – could he . . . no, he could not, he had been wrong to attempt the stone, logic and conscious effort had seduced, he came back to the strip of red carpet and discovered that he was dancing upon it. . . . He danced on.   (xxxiii, 283)

As this blur of sentences suggests, vision in India has little to do with either climax or closure, completeness being simply the product of the same subjective, emotional shift that converts muddle to mystery. In fact the festival as a whole, as a process of collective ecstasy, is without an 'emotional centre' and finishes in 'unsatisfactory and undramatic tangles' (xxxvi, 310).

It may be illuminating to compare the syntax of Godbole's dance to some sentences that render such a thematically resonant event in *Howards End*. When Margaret and Helen Schlegel take their shelter for one night in Howards End, they are able to renew their intimacy and enjoy the rewards of allegiance to the 'inner life' (xxxvii, 296).

The present flowed by them like a stream. The tree rustled. It had made music before they were born, and would continue after their deaths, but its song was of the moment. The moment had passed. The tree rustled again. Their senses were sharpened, and they seemed to apprehend life. Life passed. The tree rustled again.   (xl, 312)

This succession of simple clauses would seem to have declined the intellectual sophistication of hypotaxis, to be approaching stylistically the multiplying co-ordination of Godbole's dance. Yet the difference in effect is radical. Despite the emphasis on 'connecting' in *Howards End*, the economy and discipline of these sentences seem to insist on a sharp line between chaos and vision. Punctuation is tight; there are no detours into dependent structures. Set against the more abundant, chaotic process of the Hindu festival, the sentence 'Life passed' suggests how rigid and exclusive that line may become in *Howards End*. Finally, the image which embodies this transcendent experience, an image which Margaret, awakening at midnight, witnesses from an upstairs window, is one of clarity and stasis:

> The house had enshadowed the tree at first, but as the moon rose higher the two disentangled, and were clear for a few moments at midnight.   (p. 312)

Margaret sees; Godbole dances. Margaret achieves a heightened power of discrimination; Godbole participates in the power of indiscriminate loving. Margaret's effort is to sort things out, into orderly sentences. Godbole's is to include everything in an endless sentence.

The comma splice does more, however, than approximate immediate experience at its emotional extremes, thus suggesting the immanence of mystery in muddle. Compared to syntactical alternatives that integrate sets of elements through subordination, spliced clauses can appear as separate, impenetrable worlds. As Ronnie discovers when he tries to settle the Mohurram dispute by rerouting a procession or shortening a tower, 'the Mohammedans offered the former, the Hindus insisted on the latter' (*PI*, viii, 110). In the linking of concrete details, the splice seems to sharpen their discreteness:

> The trees were full of glossy foliage and slim green fruit, the tanks slumbered.   (xxv, 235)

> A sentry slept in the Guest House porch, lamps burned in the cruciform of the deserted rooms.   (xxxvi, 302)

> Thorns scratched the keel, they ran into an islet and startled some cranes.   (p. 307)

Each splice seems to reinforce the separateness of things and people that India decrees in her hundred voices. At the same time, the splice points towards a unity beyond, or maybe among, all the hard, disparate parts. When Ronnie leaves Fielding's party in a huff,

> there was a moment of absolute silence. No ripple disturbed the water, no leaf stirred.   (vii, 96)

The positive absence of motion, for horizontal water and vertical trees, seems suddenly to join them into one coalescence. In a more tactile way, as Aziz's friends tumble out of his bungalow into the heat,

> the space between them and their carriages, instead of being empty, was clogged with a medium that pressed against their flesh, the carriage cushions scalded their trousers, their eyes pricked, domes of hot water accumulated under their headgear and poured down their cheeks.   (x, 126)

In these spliced clauses we find the disconnected symptoms of one implicit fact: the April sun is overpowering the earth. In Forster's commitment to splices, then, there is detectable an issue central to his novel's theme. Juxtaposition begins to suggest identity, and, just as the syntax of chaos may become the syntax of ecstasy, multiplicity and unity may coexist. Perhaps the most charming image of this paradox explores its social dimension. On the return from the picnic,

> Mrs Moore slept, swaying against the rods of the howdah, Mohammed Latif embraced her with efficiency and respect. . . .   (xvi, 170)

Here people rather than things are afforded Forster's contiguous treatment. They are definitely each alone, yet tenuously together.

One last recurrence in *A Passage to India* dramatises stylistically this paradoxical affirmation of both the separateness and unity of things. Another version of strained co-ordination – and sympathetic to the dangling addition – the unwieldly catalogue erupts in the narrative to assert the irrepressibility of life against the tidiness of sentences. Two characteristics of the catalogue in *A Passage to India* invite thematic insight into the extraordinary world of that novel. Of the seven catalogues, first of all, that function as the direct objects of verbs (and persons), all but one enumerate things with illusory status. As Aziz returns from his picnic, he surveys the landscape from atop the rented elephant, 'a Mogul emperor who had done his duty'.

> he watched the Marabar Hills recede, and saw again, as

provinces of his kingdom, the grim untidy plain, the frantic
and feeble movements of the buckets, the white shrines, the
shallow graves, the suave sky, the snake that looked like a
tree.   (xvi, 169)

But at the very moment of this complacent vision, Adela is
making the deposition that will shatter Aziz's 'kingdom'. In fact,
the description within the catalogue betrays its own
unmanageability: untidy, frantic, shallow, and with that protean
snake. Also in catalogue form are the tongue-tying places Mrs
Moore 'would never visit' (xxiii, 214) and the various
performances the Rajah *would have* witnessed if he had not died
the night before the final ceremony. One object catalogue
stands out for its deceptive air of things competently
reconstructed – McBryde's account of the happenings at the
Caves:

> he spoke of Miss Derek's arrival, of the scramble down the
> gully, of the return of the two ladies to Chandrapore, and of
> the document Miss Quested signed on her arrival, in which
> mention was made of the field-glasses.   (xxiv, 226)

Actually, the methodical calmness of this catalogue, the careful
parallelism, the passively appended field glasses make all the
more ironic the discrepancy between 'circumstantial evidence'
and inscrutable reality. The issue is again illusion. And the
point, perhaps, of all these direct object catalogues – the error of
suppressing the agency and power of 'things', of the Other, of
objective experience, which is fate.
    But, most frequently, the catalogue in *A Passage to India*
functions as an appositive, giving nouns the freedom to
multiply, and one thing to lead to another. As the picnic starts
out,

> much had still to enter the purdah carriage – a box bound with
> brass, a melon wearing a fez, a towel containing guavas, a
> step-ladder and a gun.   (xiii, 142)

There is the sense here, in the relative weakness of the word
'much' balanced against its concrete particulars, of a general
category falling into its components, threatening the very

processes of generalisation, categorisation. There is the same implication in the confusion that follows the trial, when Adela is carried out into the streets of Chandrapore:

> The faint, indescribable smell of the bazaars invaded her, sweeter than a London slum, yet more disquieting: a tuft of scented cotton wool, wedged in an old man's ear, fragments of pan between his black teeth, odorous powders, oils – the Scented East of tradition, but blended with human sweat, as if a great king had been entangled in ignominy and could not free himself, or as if the heat of the sun had boiled and fried all the glories of the earth into a single mess.   (xxv, 233)

The category 'smell' at the beginning of this passage is only briefly adequate to classify the following appositives: tufts of wool, pan, powders, oils. Then a second attempt to generalise, 'the Scented East of tradition', must be adjusted by a further concrete, 'human sweat', and by two similes, the second of which finally resolves the particulars of the catalogue into perhaps the only generalisation possible of Forster's India, a sensuous 'mess'.

Yet while many catalogues dramatise the stubborn diversity of things, of experience, they may also conjure up images of unity, by seeming to enumerate the terms of an infinite equation in which everything is equal to every other thing, and ultimately equal to God. In the appositive catalogue, each developing noun is linked to the primary noun, and by analogy to each other noun:

> The signs of the contented Indian evening multiplied: frogs on all sides, cow-dung burning eternally; a flock of belated hornbills overhead, looking like winged skeletons as they flapped across the gloaming.   (xxxvi, 302)

Signs = frogs = cow = dung = hornbills. This sense of a mystical equation emerges finally from what can be read as two sets of posterior appositives to the noun 'God Himself':

> Thus was He thrown year after year, and were others thrown – little images of Ganpati, baskets of ten-day corn, tiny tazias after Mohurram – scapegoats, husks, emblems of passage. (p. 309)

Cosmic homogeneity is solidly realised, though inverted, in the message Mrs Moore hears in the cave: 'Pathos, piety, courage – they exist, but are identical, and so is filth. Everything exists, nothing has value' (xiv, 160). A second anterior appositive reiterates this theme: 'Hope, politeness, the blowing of a nose, the squeak of a boot, all produce "boum" ' (p. 159). In the 'Temple' section, 'boum' becomes 'Radhadkrishna' or 'God si love', and the negative proposition of the caves is modified to affirm that everything exists, everything may have divine value. It is with a last anterior–appositive catalogue, though, that Forster reminds us that the moment with God, when the universal equation receives its completing central term, is brief. And, just as 'it becomes history and falls under the rule of time', so must the friendship of Aziz and Fielding succumb to the India of separate and disparate pieces, united only in denial:

> the temples, the tank, the jail, the palace, the birds, the carrion, the Guest house, that came into view as they issued from the gap and saw Mau beneath: they didn't want it, they said in their hundred voices, 'No, not yet', and the sky said, 'No, not there.'   (xxxvii, 316)

It is this India, of autonomous things, insoluble muddle, that strained and perhaps finally defeated the complex sentences of E. M. Forster the novelist.

7 The Spirit behind the Frieze?

JOHN DREW

In *A Passage to India*, the poet – for there is one in E. M. Forster – identifies himself wholly with Professor Godbole. Whatever difficulties are experienced by the other characters are a direct result of their failure to live life according to Godbole's philosophy and the action of the novel, which stems from their inadequacies, is an exposition of this truth. It is the passages where Godbole briefly appears which give rise to the music that Forster suggests reverberates in the mind when the reading of a good novel is over and allows the novel a dimension which is not only larger than life but also, paradoxically, larger than literature. The further question of whether Godbole can embrace not simply the other characters but even 'birds, caves, railways and the stars' may be resolved as much as it ever can when it is understood that, faced with this issue, Forster is left confronting not the limitations of Godbole so much as the limitations of the novel. In so far as the novel form permits him to, Forster the poet identifies himself wholly with Godbole.

From the time of Alexander the Great, India has been associated in the European mind with the philosophic life and it is therefore not surprising to find that philosophy provides the most coherent approach to *A Passage to India*. The philosophy the Greeks saw practised in India they likened to that of Pythagoras and Plato[1] and the respectful attitude of the Neo-Platonists to India[2] encouraged later European Orientalists to single out the mystical Vedanta as India's principal philosophical system and to discover an almost total identity between it and Neo-Platonism.[3] Shortly before publishing his Indian novel, Forster subscribed quite consciously to this conception and shortly afterwards he used the Neo-Platonist intellectual scheme as it had been elaborated by Coleridge and Shelley to explain the imaginative or magical experience at the heart of literature. Since India has made an exploration of states of consciousness central to its culture, it is not surprising that Forster found it to be the most appropriate image for the passage to the Imagination – and perhaps to an even more mystical state in which (according to Shelley – *Prometheus Unbound*, ii.iv. 116) the deep truth is imageless.

It is in *Alexandria: A History and a Guide*, published in 1922, that Forster likens Neo-Platonism to Indian thought, especially in its promise that a man shall be (and not merely see) God.[4] He mentions that, whether or not a direct Hindu influence was at work, numerous parallels exist between the two. This remark is important from the man then writing his novel on India because he suggests that Alexandria produced nothing greater than the *Enneads* of Plotinus, the central text of Neo-Platonism (part of a translation and a summary of which he had just been reading).[5] Forster observes that there is an antithetical movement in the *Enneads* as they deal first with the emanation of creation (as it were) out of God and then with its striving to return. He describes the three hypostases (or progressive emanations) of God as, first, the Unity about which nothing can be predicated, including even Its existence, and which is good only as the goal of all striving; secondly, the Intellectual Principle, or Mind, containing all thought of all things; and third, the All Soul, or conceptions of gods, animals, plants and stones graspable by the senses, with matter ('which seems so important to us') being the last and feeblest emanation. At this point creative power comes to a halt. Forster suggests that this scheme may appear abstruse and less attractive than what he calls the more emotional (properly, devotional) side of the *Enneads*, which speaks of the striving of all parts of God, even the stones, to realise their divine potential, something finally achieved only in an abstract (i.e. concentrated and imageless) state apprehended by way of the mystic Vision.

Forster is not the first artist who has been attracted to the *Enneads* for their mystical assertion that matter becomes insubstantial upon recognition of the true spiritual nature of life. Before I argue that this scheme and even the antithetical pattern of the *Enneads* is inherent in *A Passage to India*, I should like to demonstrate simply (though much more crudely than Coleridge or Shelley) the more general applicability of Neo-Platonism to our reading of literature. The theory of the three hypostases (or, as they are seen to be, successive levels of consciousness) suggests that the literary work is more fully realised the closer it gets to the mystic Vision. At the least level of achievement there is the work whose images remain disparate, differentiated, fragmented, multiple and as subject to change and chance as anything in the phenomenal world is to ordinary sight. According to this view, an imagist approach to literature would not be highly regarded, since the purpose of the work should be to locate the Unity which underlies diversity, the One which holds together the many and allows the poet quite spontaneously to discover the common identity of unlike images. In the fully realised work the images are indivisible though multiple, the One and the many, the ἐν καὶ πᾶν.

It might be supposed that by its very nature literature cannot go further than this into some abstract region indefinable in words. In fact, in his critical writings in the mid 1920s, Forster himself suggested that it could and that there are works which not only outstrip others but outstrip even themselves. In the Clark Lectures of 1927 (published as *Aspects of the Novel*), Forster refers (ii, 26; viii, 113–16) to this quality in terms of music: others have preferred to speak in terms of magic. Forster is aware that the Neo-Platonists excluded from their writings all references to daily life and that a novelist can (or could then) hardly be expected to do this. None the less, in his lectures he regrets the material stuff of the novel as much as he says Plotinus regretted having a body, and the whole thrust of his critical no less than his imaginative writing is towards as much of an affirmation of the mystic Vision as the negative theology will allow. His perceptive comment that the Neo-Platonists were not the disembodied spirits their writings might make them seem but very much human is dependent, I think, on his seeing that their striving for Vision did not constitute a rejection of the ordinary world but an attempt to find the principle which alone could give value to everything within it. For this reason, if we are to read *A Passage to India* in terms of Neo-Platonism, the novel may be taken as a comment on its own nature even while it comments on the nature of the universe.

If we are to argue that Neo-Platonism is the key to an

understanding of Forster's Hindus and Forster's Hindus are the key to an understanding of his novel, then the argument is going to have to turn very largely on Godbole, and this not in spite of but precisely *because of* the fact that he is largely absent from the book. Of course Godbole *is* a trifle absurd and Forster will not be taken very seriously when he says that it is in his purple macaroni turban and socks patterned with clocks that he reconciles the products of East and West (vii, 89). But then Forster does make the point that, according to the Hindu view, God, being all-inclusive, participates in practical joking no less than in seriousness (xxxiii, 286) and Forster himself goes on less whimsically to add that the harmony Godbole suggests is 'mental as well as physical'. In fact, it is not in Godbole's wardrobe so much as in his philosophy (which may look equally absurd) that the real harmony between East and West is effected.

Some of Forster's readers may well feel with Fielding that one of the most frustrating moments in the novel comes when Godbole denies that he is competent to judge whether or not the Marabar expedition has been a catastrophe and whether or not Aziz is innocent (xix, 183–7). As far as Godbole is concerned, legal evidence determines matters of guilt and innocence, but society's laws are no more ultimate than the personal opinion he refuses to give: both are grounded on a faith in individual perceptions. According to his philosophy, good and evil are not performed in isolation by an individual – they express the whole of the universe. The difference between them, he explains, is that the Lord is either present or absent – but that even His absence implies His presence. To the European ear this may sound mystifyingly Indian. In fact the words are virtually those of Plotinus in the *Enneads* (vi.ix. 4) when he makes the distinction that God, though everywhere present, is absent from all save those who through a kindred power within themselves may see in so far as God may at all be seen.[6] This remark, for Plotinus as for Godbole, comes as part of a larger argument that each several thing in the Cosmos is affected by all else and that Life does not look to the individual but to the whole. In that individual souls are one with the Soul of the Universe, we participate in good: in that we are embodied we all share in the evil abroad in the universe (*Enneads*, iv.iv.32, ix.1; vi.ii.21, iii.9).

It is this cosmic and impersonal standpoint which provides

the philosophical explanation for Godbole's song at the tea party that had proved so baffling to the guests there. Just as Plotinus, in a central passage on the One Life (vi.v.12), asserts that the All does not have to come and be present to those who have turned away, so does Godbole explain that Lord Krishna, Indian epitome of the All, neglects or refuses to come: it is we who have to go to Krishna or rather, non-dualistically, take on the form of Krishna and assimilate ourselves to Him (*PI*, vii, 96; xxxiii, 287; xxxvi, 299).

Fielding, exasperated as he is by (what is to his rational perception) Godbole's obtuseness about the Marabars, none the less still wants to have Godbole's opinion about the moral propriety of his resignation from the club (xxi, 198). Godbole's philosophy may be baffling but he attracts the sort of instinctive trust which Plotinus makes a prerequisite for Vision (xix, 184; *Enneads*, vi.ix.4). On first meeting him, we learn that, whereas for him tranquillity appears to swallow up everything, the rest of the characters have no reserve of tranquillity to draw upon (*PI*, vii, 94–5). 'Tranquillity' is the term used in the *Enneads* to describe the contemplative state the sage must realise if he is to be Vision itself (iii.viii.6): Neo-Platonism advocates precisely the kind of abstract thought which, we are told, an encounter with Godbole's mind will evoke (*PI*, vii, 92). For Godbole, as for the ideal sage of the *Enneads*, happiness consists not in action but in wisdom (i.v.10).[7]

The most strenuous action performed by Godbole in the earlier part of the novel is the singing of the song at the tea party (*PI*, vii, 95–6). To this song may be traced the whole curious course of events thereafter. The song enables us to explain why there would have been no story without it and why the novel we do have, like Godbole himself, slips off just when it seems to be most needed – its words, like those Godbole himself might have uttered at the trial, lacking both basis and conclusion and floating through the air (xix, 183; xxi, 198). The song consists of a series of sounds unrelated to known forms of music and it is superseded by an absolute stillness. A study of music may tell us something about the nature of Godbole's song and so may a study of poetry and philosophy. Yet it is none of these. It is the song not of a nightingale (or bulbul of Persian poetry – ix, 119; xxx, 264; xxxiv, 290) but of an unknown bird and reaches into that silence to which music, poetry and philosophy can all point, being as they are the beauty which is the bloom upon truth. But however elusive the nature of the song itself, its effect within the novel is quite precise. It has been a call to Vision to all those present and they ignore it at their spiritual peril.

Specifically, Godbole's song has been a call to the slumbering spirit, registering only the distinction between pleasure and pain, to break out (like Psyche) from its cocoon of self-enthralment and social endeavour (xiv, 145–6).[8] Speaking to Fielding later, Adela makes the point that the song had left her living at half pressure and suggests that it had exposed the inadequacy of her personal life (xxvi, 240). As a result of this, she develops an irritation against Ronny which is really against herself, breaks off her engagement before animal contact restores it (viii, 97, 99, 101, 108–9; xxviii, 256) and, still aware that her life is all out of proportion and that there is something to which she has not been attentive enough, goes ill equipped into the cave (xv, 162–4; xxiv, 215–16, 229; xxix, 260–1). While Adela resents the apathy which overtakes her after the song has exposed her spiritual inadequacy, Mrs Moore accepts hers. Even before she has heard the song, India has impressed upon her that, though we must insist that God is Love, God is not to be either so easily located or so readily summoned as Christianity would have us believe (v, 71). She has become aware of the silence which exists beyond the remotest echo and is therefore more attuned to the ostensibly negative song Godbole sings. After hearing it she is no longer so committed to the social conviction that has brought her to India – namely, that marriage is efficacious (viii, 109–10) – and on the day of the Marabar expedition she even senses that marriage might actually be a bar to man's happiness, an idea which strikes her in the image of a person trying to take hold of her hand (xiv, 147–8). That idea is personified in the novel as Godbole and, metaphorically speaking, if any character may be said to offer his hand (and mind) to Mrs Moore it is Godbole.

An explanation of why the two English ladies have been wrong-footed by India may be offered by reading one incident on the journey to the Marabars in terms of the *Enneads*. The sunrise fails (*PI*, xiv, 149–50). The sun, we are told, has power but no beauty, it is not the unattainable friend, the eternal promise, the never-withdrawn suggestion that haunts our consciousness (x, 127). But if virtue has appeared to fail in the celestial fount and Adela gets sunstroke it is because she has sought in the sunrise, as in India generally, something of scenic, or material, interest. Plotinus, taking the sun as an image for godhead, says that it is always difficult to tell (as it is difficult to tell approaching the Marabars) whether or not the sun has risen but that this is all the more reason to await it with tranquillity, confident that it is capable of filling the contemplating Intellect – above which alone it can dawn – with a power which is also beautiful (*Enneads*, v.v.8).[9] The women have been looking at India in the wrong way. Like Forster when he began his novel (*PI*, Introduction, p. 14), they have expected India to provide answers through its external forms (they have turned their souls outwards, as Plotinus would say) and become ensnared by the magic (or Maya) of appearances. According to Plotinus, only the Self-intent, those absorbed in inward contemplation, go free of this magic (*Enneads*, IV.iv.43–4). He specifically names caring for children and planning marriage (activities designed to establish personal relationships and ensure the regeneration of matter as it participates in human form) as examples of the bait which causes people to fall under a spell which deludes them and it is precisely these which have brought Mrs Moore and Adela to India (*PI*, iii, 46; viii, *passim*; xiv, 146–7).

Fielding also feels the effect of Godbole's song. But in spite of Godbole's prompting ('it was as if someone had told him there was such a moment'), he misses his chance of Vision (the Marabars transformed) just after he has asserted the innocence of Aziz (xx, 197).[10] The best he can do is to see the Marabars as romantic, a perception associated with the ultimately abortive pantheism of 'dearest Grasmere', as spiritually unproductive for Fielding as it has been for Ronny (viii, 99; xiv, 150; xxviii, 256; xxxii, 278). The Θεος (or One God) is not to be sought in the Παν (or All). The reflection about the true nature of the echo remains forever at the verge of Fielding's mind. Similarly, the significance of Godbole's song (the singing of which he was responsible for in the first place – v, 66), eludes him to the end, though not the recollection of it, which still preoccupies him during his final meeting with Aziz (xxxi, 272, 274; xxxvii, 313).

A Passage to India is not a humanistic novel. It reveals that the very best sort of humanism ('goodwill plus culture and intelligence' – vii, 80) is incapable of sustaining a single friendship, let alone the whole world. Forster makes the point

that Fielding, like Adela, remains a dwarf without the apparatus
for judging whether or not the hundred Indias are one
(xxix, 261–2). Once more it is Plotinus who can suggest why this
is. Fielding is an atheist (ix, 124; xxvii, 254; xxxi, 274) and,
according to the *Enneads*, the whole question of visionary
experience cannot even be discussed, with those who have
drifted far from God (vi.ix.5). If the Englishwomen are in India
to foster personal relationships, Fielding is concerned with
teaching people to be individuals and to understand other
individuals (*PI*, xi, 132–3; vii, 84). It is basic to the *Enneads*
that the individual in any form, while more readily accessible to
our cognisance, does not in fact exist (ii.i.1–2; vi.iii.9). Earlier
on, Fielding could at least say of himself that, minus the critical
holiness, he resembled a holy man in that he was not planning
marriage and so was free of the desire for possessions (*PI*,
xi, 132–3; xxvi, 242; cf. *Enneads*, i.ii.1). By the end of the
novel, however, he cannot even say that: he is married, about to
have a child and Aziz has become for him merely a memento
(*PI*, xxxvii, 313). He remains closed to the spirit of Hinduism,
ignorant of the fact that Aziz, far from being able to enlighten
him on the subject as an Oriental, will be unable to do so
precisely because he accepts that limiting definition of himself.

The mosque, we are told, also misses the universe which
Fielding has missed or rejected (xxxi, 272). Aziz traces his
culture back to the Mogul emperors, the first of whom, Babur,
found India alien (xxxvi, 301; xiv, 155; xxx, 265).[11] The
Moslems value the Plotinian secondaries of form and beauty,
the arts of architecture and poetry and the gracefulness of
speech and gesture which are 'the social equivalent of Yoga'
(xxvii, 250–1).[12] The God to which they point becomes a social
formulation, even a pun (xxxi, 272; xxxv, 292), and
consequently religious devotion is too easily reduced to the form
of personal emotion. Emotion determines the way the Moslems
use words: not literally, like the British, but as an expression of
mood, and it causes Aziz – again concerned, as Plotinus suggests
it is fatal to be, with marriage (Fielding's) – to build his life on a
mistake (xxxi, 268; 277; xxxv, 297–8).[13] Aziz is already
involved in the Islamic social obligation of caring for children
and this concern for 'the society of the future' (ii, 36, 44; xi, 130,
132) combined with his personal experience, leads him to care
for something else Plotinus asserts a wise man will ignore: the

politics of imperialism (xxx, 266; xxxiv, 290; xxxvii, 314–15).[14]

It is in the light of these and further Neo-Platonist criteria that the final ride of Aziz and Fielding may be read. In answer to the question of whether the two men can be friends, the earth, in its hundred voices, says, 'No, not yet' and – to show that the timing of their reconciliation is not, as Aziz suggests, dependent on the coming of political independence to India – the sky says, 'No, not there' (xxxvii, 316). On the face of it, Forster is being even more relentless than Kipling, who at least excepted 'strong men' from his conclusion that East and West should not meet before earth and sky stood together on Judgement Day.[15] In *Aspects of the Novel*, however, Forster insists that the chronological ending of a novel is far from being its real conclusion. He may well have had his own last novel in mind. The place which is holding Aziz and Fielding apart is diversified India, the India of a hundred voices (*PI*, xxxvii, 316).[16] To this India the two men are subject because, in direct proportion to the share of action they have in the novel, they remain ignorant of the One India. Like the hundred Krishnas of Godbole's song (vii, 96), the hundred Indias have to be apprehended as an abstract or imageless One. The One India, no less than the hundred (being inclusive of them), denies that reconciliation is to be contained in a particular time or place. Unlike the negation of the many Indias, however, that of the One (in common with the One of the *Enneads*) implies infinite possibility and does not regard time or place as ultimate. It is for this reason that Forster comes to recognise that India is not, as he had earlier supposed, a promise (that man will actually realise his divine identity with all things), but an appeal (to man to aspire towards its possibility in the abstract – xiv, 149).[17] Forster's novel, like Godbole's song, may cease upon 'the sub-dominant' but it does not conclude there.

Before considering further the hypothesis that *A Passage to India* is not so much about several Indias mutually at variance as about One India in various stages of Self-realisation, I should stress that literature, being composed of words which are images and of images which symbolise ideas, is not on the face of it mystical abstraction. If mystical experience is imageless and self-contained, then it would seem that the materials of a literary work could at best point only to the possibility of its existence. Yet it is equally true that the possibility of the existence of something abstract and self-contained can be predicated only by some form more tangible than itself. Furthermore, a mystic Vision which is all-encompassing cannot by definition exclude the ideal and imaginary world of literature. If a novel cannot contain mystical experience, it could, perhaps, by a process of assimilation, be totally transformed by it. Were this to happen to a novel, its condition, as Forster hoped, might approximate to that of poetry or music.

Godbole provides a perfect analogue for the novelist because his religious rites stand in much the same relationship to mysticism as literature may do. In a way which is not incongruous to the syncretistic Indian mind,[18] he is simultaneously an Advaitin (espousing the philosophy that there is no duality of either matter and spirit or man and God) and a *bhakta* (or religious devotee who asserts that an apprehension of total Union is actually dependent on a sense of the distinct separateness of lover and beloved). Godbole's song reconciles this apparent contradiction. He takes on the persona of a 'milkmaiden', or *gopi* (here presumably Radha), who calls on Krishna to come to her only and so be united in love. Short of being granted such an exclusively personal relationship, she implores Krishna to multiply himself a hundredfold and appear to others as well as to herself (vii, 96). But, as Godbole explains to Mrs Moore, Krishna does not come in this, or any other, song. According to Godbole's philosophy, if a second distinct image appeared, it would circumscribe the infinite potential of an abstract, or mystical, One. His song remains one of pure aspiration.

Because *bhakti* cuts the Gordian knot of metaphysics and uses images of separateness, and especially that of separated lovers, it may be particularly appealing to a novelist, whose novel must necessarily live among the manifold and diverse images of the world and whose theme, according to Forster, is invariably that of love (*AN*, iii, 34–5, 37–8). It should be noticed, however, that *bhakti* is no less abstruse than the Advaita in that, in this context at least, it uses the image of separateness to indicate not actual separateness but, on the contrary, potential Union. For its part, although it forswears duality, Advaita can depict Absolute Reality only in terms of a realm of relative reality.[19] Plotinus, likewise, has to resort to imagery drawn from the sensible world in order to indicate the nature of the Intellectual. Moreover, as Forster notes, Plotinus, by virtue of his profession as philosopher, has to indicate the comprehensiveness of mystical experience by means of an elaboration of the gradations of matter. Forster is particularly sensitive to this since, by virtue of his profession, he too uses language as the material medium through which to discover the comprehensive nature of Reality. As both Plotinus and Forster are aware, the capacity of any sort of material, including language, to do this can be gauged only by the extent to which it has been transformed into something relatively immaterial, or insubstantial, a quality perhaps reflected in Forster's description of the Hindu festival, which, he says, has an emotional centre as impossible to locate as the heart of a cloud (*PI*, xxxvi, 310).

If, for the *bhakta*, God's presence not only is but can only be implied through absence, so for the novelist, the immaterial (or aethereal) not only is but *can* only be implied through the material. Forster, like the *bhakta*, uses images of separateness to imply not separateness but potential Unity. He is as abstruse as he says Plotinus is. It is not simply that in *A Passage to India* nightmare implies vision and disillusionment implies enlightenment; it is that in each case the former is a necessary concomitant of the latter. The way in which an opened Marabar cave points on to the abstract conception of an absolute void represented by an unopened cave (xii, 139) forces us to conceive of Absolute Reality in terms of something more abstract than the images in Godbole's Vision (or those in Forster's novel). The Caves may be regarded not as a negation of Vision but as a necessary postulate of it, indicating not the primacy of matter but the non-exclusive (and therefore potentially all-inclusive) nature of Spirit.

Even by those who are prepared to concede to Godbole a paramount place in the novel, the Caves are frequently seen as offering a challenge too great to be contained by him. He is silenced by mention of them and does not confront them physically. Matter, so the argument runs, has proved too intransigent for even Godbole's refined consciousness. At the heart of things, there is only a meaningless void. If a Marabar cave is subjected to the same sort of Neo-Platonist reading we gave the sun rising over the Marabars, however, we shall see that the Marabars have only as much power as is permitted them by the perceptions of the onlookers. Neo-Platonist philosophy, far from ignoring the problems posed by materialism, expressly exists to confront and incorporate (or, rather, refine and aetherealise) them. Plotinus, like Forster, uses the imagery of a sterile and unproductive land to describe spiritual desolation (*Enneads*, vi.iii.8; cf. *PI*, viii, 102–3; xiv, 152) and, following Plato's great myth, constantly uses imagery evocative of the Cave to suggest the deceptive appearance of matter. Matter, he says, is like a mirror showing things when they are really elsewhere, containing nothing but pretending everything. Precisely because it has no form or reality of its own are we deceived by the apparent authenticity of its reflections. But it has no power of retention and if things appear to originate in it, that is only because whatever confronts it is repelled by it. This repulsion he likens to echoes being flung back from a repercussive plane surface. Were the whole earth not aspirant, matter would be capable only of coiling about in circuit (*Enneads*, iii.vi.7, 13–14; iv.iv.16; cf. *PI*, xiv, 158–9).

Forster's conception of a Marabar cave is, I would have thought, extraordinarily consistent with this description of matter as a void which at the moment it is first penetrated by form takes on the appearance of a mirror which mimics, lies, repels, coils and throws back an echo in such a way as to suggest it has inherent properties of its own. Be that as it may, there still remains the question whether Forster's Marabars can be dismissed quite so totally as Plotinus dismisses matter. At the opening of the 'Caves' section of his novel, for example, Forster envisages the world before the advent of the gods, when it was pure matter, older than all spirit. But, then, Plotinus is equally capable of conceiving of the universe as stark body, the blankness of matter and the absence of Being (*Enneads*, v.i.2; cf. *PI*, xii, 137–8). For him, matter is essential evil, authentic non-existence, and it is only when it is perceived that it pretends to a participation in Being it does not really have, its existence being but a pale reflection and less complete than that of the things implanted in it (*Enneads*, ii.iv.10–16, v. 2–5; vi.iii.7). If an unopened Marabar cave appears to be the centre of a wholly material universe, it may be remembered that the extreme idealist position, which denies any reality to the effect, is so perfectly the converse of materialism, which denies any reality to the cause, that their terminology is identical: the Essential Existence of Plotinus is defined wholly in terms of negatives. Not surprisingly, Plotinus warns us that unless we turn appearances about we shall be left void of God (*Enneads*, v.v.11).[20]

This need to turn appearances about is equally pertinent to a reading of *A Passage to India*: the peculiar train of events in the novel does not make coherent sense until we do so. Godbole is not, as it appears, being perverse when he refuses to admit that the visit to the Marabars has been unsuccessful. Like Plotinus, he believes that most or even all forms of evil serve the universe (*Enneads*, ii.iii.18). The caves have actually provided the non-Hindus who visit them with an opportunity to confront their spiritual limitations. After her visit to them, Mrs Moore, for example, concludes (exactly contrary to the *Enneads*) that matter alone has existence and that it is from the huge scenic background of the heavens that all magnitude has passed (*PI*, xxiii, 212–13; cf. *Enneads*, iii.vi.16).[21] Yet she understands that nothing evil (in the Christian sense) has been in the cave (*PI*, xiv, 159). She has experienced the emptiness of the universe and concluded that God is non-existent in it. She is totally disillusioned with marriage, love and all personal relationships. Yet her tirade on this subject (picked up as 'sounds' by a Hindu *mali* outside) is the basis for Adela's moment of Vision at the trial (xxii, 207–9; xxiv, 221, 227),[22] and for the deification of Mrs Moore herself. The cynicism it expresses about any form of personal relationship provides an impersonal perspective on anything Adela supposes might have happened to her, whether in a cave with Aziz or in a church with Ronny. For the first time Adela doubts if any other person was involved in the experience which had resulted from her going into the cave bored with sight-seeing, doubting the propriety of her own marriage and asking Aziz an unconsciously offensive question about his.

For her part, Mrs Moore has completely cut adrift from the personal values she hitherto brought to her social and religious life, has broken out the cocoon which had enveloped her; her former life has become a dream and she has laid herself open to the Impersonalism which not only promises nothing, but in its earlier stages is likely to be as productive of nightmare as of vision (xiv, 147, 160–1; xxiii, 212–13). While she did not hear Godbole explain to Fielding the meaning of God's absence, she heard him express the same thing in a different way at the tea party; she will experience (or at least bear out) the truth of the same remark at the Marabar trial, where her own absence proves to be a more powerful psychical presence than her physical presence could ever have been;[23] and, become at that time part of a god (xxiv, 228; xxviii, 255),[24] she will be further impelled to that place where completeness is found when she impinges on Godbole's consciousness during the visionary frenzy at Mau (xxxiii, 283, 287).

While there is insufficient space here to develop in detail the argument in favour of a Neo-Platonist reading of the novel, one further concept is vitally necessary for anyone wishing to follow it through. According to the *Enneads*, the universe is ensouled, an idea so abstract that for purposes of discussion we have to image out the soul in terms of sight (Vision) or, as Plotinus prefers, sound. The Universal Soul, or Cosmic Sound, is all-pervasive. Once again, we are asked to turn appearances about. God is not in space, as art depicts: space is in God (*Enneads*, vi.viii.11).[25] Strictly speaking, God knows no partition and it is as much an illusion of the corporeal realm to say that a soul (like Mrs Moore's) is part of a god (worshipped in particular forms at particular places) as to say that it is individual. It is true, however, that in its upward striving the partial accepts the working of the entire upon the entire only partially at first, though the entire enters later (iv.iii.20; vi.iv.14, v.4–5). There are two phases of the soul: the lower, tied to sense impressions; and the higher, freed of them. When the soul is set on self (that is, on individuality and personality) it produces its lower, an image of itself, a non-being, which leaves it wandering into the void. A soul may liberate itself from this descent and become illuminated by assimilating itself to the soul above it. The lower phase of the soul then merges with the higher, the shadow or echo that it is no longer enjoying the substantiality it appeared to have (iii.ix.2; iv.iii.31).

This conception may provide an explanation both for the shadow which bottles Adela up in the cave and for the Vision which comes to her in court following the cessation of the chanting of Mrs Moore's name and of her own insidious echo (evil reflection as that is of her own self-centred thoughts). Adela's higher, or impersonal, soul has been assimilated to the new-found Impersonalism of Mrs Moore above it; her lower, or personal, soul which in the cave took the cosmic personally is no longer dominant but subordinate – and so Aziz does not appear in the cave. The difficulty for the novelist, of course, is to find some way of depicting these subtle spiritual forces at work in the universe. No wonder Forster regretted that the novel had to tell a story (*AN*, ii, 17, 29). In fact *A Passage to India* follows Plotinus in using the imagery of a Cosmic Sound audible to those receptive enough to let the hearings of sense go by and keep the soul's perception open to sounds from above (*Enneads*, IV.iv.40; v.i.12; VI.iv.12, 15). Sometimes the sounds (Forster calls them 'messages from another world' – *PI*, xxix, 262) become as distinct as the name of Mrs Moore, which when chanted by the Hindus not only helps Adela to be rid of her echo and attain Vision but also helps Mrs Moore herself further along the road of spiritual enlightenment (to which, as Plotinus says, death is no barrier – *Enneads*, IV.vii.15, 20). Moreover, Forster allows this invisible (or inaudible) power quite practical effects. Through it physical pain may be eliminated and the might of an empire undermined.

It is also the sound of Mrs Moore's name which permits Aziz to partake in the spiritual growth it represents. The belief in ghosts which he denies verbally but which runs in his blood was evoked by Mrs Moore's first appearance in the mosque (*PI*, ii, 42) and sustains his faith in her long after she has abandoned him to the fateful cave and their personal friendship is over (xiv, 161; xxii, 210).[26] He fancies she is present at the trial (xxvii, 252), it is on account of her that he renounces his claim against Adela for compensation (xxix, 259), and when, after that, he opts, like Akbar, to accommodate himself to Hindu India (xxxv, 292), he remains open to those intimations from the Unseen which cause him to love not emotionally but in an impersonal way. Hearing the chant of the Hindu crowd at Mau (which combines the two names, Radha and Krishna, which remained separate in Godbole's original song), Aziz identifies it with the chant of the Hindus during his trial, and this revival of the name of Mrs Moore causes him to change his attitude to her son Ralph (xxxvi, 305–8).[27] Finally, unlike Fielding, he is responsive to the even more subtle prompting – in his case 'not a sight, but a sound' – which flits past him and causes him to promise Adela he will associate her thereafter with the irreproachable Mrs Moore (xxxvii, 314).

Plotinus suggests that even forms of life which are receptive to a significant, or sacred, sound, do not necessarily apprehend the significance of it (*Enneads*, VI.iv.15).[28] Aziz, for example, can

revere the name of Mrs Moore without knowing why (*PI*,
xxvii, 253; xxxvi, 306) and the sound of it has a partial but not a
total effect on him. He perceives that she has penetrated to the
Orient (ii, 45; xxvii, 253; xxxvi, 306).[29] In fact Mrs Moore has
penetrated further than the Orient (presupposing as that does,
dualistically, a separate Occident) and it is only the Hindus who
perceive that she has penetrated to the silence and nothingness
which underlie the universe. Contemplative and disinclined to
action, the Hindus are not such stuff as novels are made of. For
the most part in *A Passage to India* they stand as still and silent
figures as in a frieze (iii, 49; v, 66), like the water-chestnut
gatherer and the punkah wallah and the servitor. Yet these
figures, as elusive as the Hindu sound to which they are the
visual equivalent, as distinct as the forms of the chant and yet as
undifferentiated, personify collectively, as Godbole does
individually, the spirit behind the frieze.

    Forster takes a cosmic view of the Hindu social system and, in
so doing, reflects what Plotinus has to say about the way Unity
takes on the aspect of diversity when it fissures into universality:
Hinduism is compared to the Indian soil, the fissures of which
are infinite and yet all part of a totality (xxxiv, 289; *Enneads*,
III.iii.1). In their festival the Hindus, themselves grading and
drifting beyond the (merely) educated vision (*PI*, iv, 57–8),[30] seek
through a mystical inner state not only to embrace all that is in
India but to make that passage to more than India which
Whitman refers to as the secret of the earth and sky.[31] The final
injunction of the *Enneads* that the mystic must leave 'the temple
images behind' receives outward ceremonial expression in the
Hindu procession to the lake at Mau. There earth and sky lean
together about to 'clash in ecstasy' and eventually a wild tempest
engulfs people of all religions alike. Forster is not being ironic in
a superficial way when he tells us that the emotional centre of all
this can be located no more than can the heart of a cloud. What
he is really pointing to may be suggested by a passage in Plotinus
where the radiance within the enlightened soul is compared to
the light of a lantern 'when fierce gusts beat about it in a turmoil
of wind and tempest' (*Enneads*, I.iv.8; cf. terminology here with
PI, xxxvi, 309). The Hindu servitor who presides at the lake,
being the spot of filth without which the spirit cannot cohere, has
an authority more subtle than that of the rajah, just as the
authority of the punkah wallah in the court is subtler than that of

the magistrate and the sensibility of the water-chestnut gatherer as subtle as that of the Brahmin Godbole.[32] Capable of confounding every social distinction, together this triad composes a single archetypal god, emerging, re-emerging and being submerged to the accompaniment of that chain of sacred sounds which, first heard in Godbole's song and then again at the trial, reverberates with enough effect at Mau for us to suppose that this is the cosmic thread upon which the elements of the novel are strung.

The description of the festival at Mau is a literary attempt to depict what Plotinus tried to reflect in philosophy: the mystic Vision. It appears to be the climax of the novel and yet, if the novel is to sustain our philosophical reading, this is not so: India does not positively admit of a climax (xxxvi, 310). Why not? Because none can say when and where the mystic Vision has been achieved: it does not fall under the rules of place any more than of time (xxxiii, 285)[33] and, in the event of its achievement, it will cover not just the part but the whole, entire. None the less, in so far as any onlooker can ever know, it seems that the Hindu villagers at Mau, in an orgy not of the body but of the spirit, have become Love and do enjoy the mystic Vision. In terminology which appears to derive directly from the *Enneads*, Forster describes how a glimpse of Krishna brings into the faces of the villagers a radiance and a beauty about which there is nothing personal since it causes them to resemble one another during the moment of its indwelling (*PI*, xxxiii, 281–2).[34] The qualification that the onlooker never can know when the mystic Vision has been achieved is taken to a further abstract level when Forster interjects to say that even the adept himself does not know (p. 285). This remark is pertinent to what happens to Godbole at the festival.

The argument that the Hindus embrace all else in the novel and that the poetic Forster is to be wholly identified with Godbole might be thought to depend on our certainty that Godbole has enjoyed a complete Vision. Yet Godbole's Vision appears to be abortive. Godbole's soul is 'a tiny reverberation', part of the chain of sacred sounds which evoke Vision. At Mau, certain definite images impinge on his memory and he remembers, in a progressive descent through creation, Mrs Moore, a wasp and a stone, images which the novel has already linked in a chain of association. At that point, Godbole is returned to his immediate environment and we are told that he had been wrong to attempt the stone, that he had been seduced by logic and conscious effort (pp. 282–4). What has gone wrong? Has Godbole's philosophy failed him and thus invalidated our reading of the novel in terms of it? If Plotinus is to continue to be our guide, it will be seen that it is not the philosophy which has proved inadequate. In a central passage on the nature of the One Life, Plotinus speaks of that Intellectual, or Imaginative, state where the one soul holds within it all souls, or intelligences, with every item standing forth distinctly, multiple yet indivisible (*Enneads*, vi.iv.14, ix.5) But, he says (and the but is very important), this association of item after item is not identity and the soul must speed to 'something greater to its memory' which acts not by seeing and knowing but by loving. For that the lover must elaborate within himself an immaterial image, the soul must be kept formless (v.iii.17; vi.vii.22, 33–5, ix.4). Godbole allowed himself to be distracted by his religious duties, by externals: the need for a new hymn and the readjustment of his pince-nez. Plotinus specifically warns against 'throwing outward' during the looking (vi.ix.7). It is precisely the tiny fragments of Godbole's consciousness that attend to 'outside things' which permit 'tiny splinters of detail', distinct images, to emerge from the imageless Vision, or 'universal warmth'. Thereafter item can follow item, however affirmative the understanding, and ultimately one image will prove exclusive of the rest.

The image which proves resistant to Godbole is stone, and it is consistent with Plotinus to say that this is because stone, the mineral by which the void of a Marabar cave is contained, is of all creation the least aspirant. It does not follow from this, however, that any inherent power should be attributed to stone or that we should see the Marabars as weighing anything in the balance against Godbole's philosophy. Plotinus himself explains that you cannot use a stone by way of contrast to the One since the One is wholly free of attributes and qualities (vi.v.11–12).[35] It is fallacious ever to conceive of the metaphysical in terms of the physical. Spirit operates by way of all conceivable principles but lies outside them all and encompasses them all. For this reason Plotinus says, 'Seeking Him, seek nothing of Him outside: within is to be sought what follows upon Him: Himself do not attempt' (vi.viii.18). Godbole should not have 'attempted' stone not only because stone is the physical ultimately most resistant to absorption into the metaphysical, but also because the metaphysical Ultimate, which alone could absorb it, should not be attempted. The ultimate Vision (i.e. Union) will not be achieved by conscious effort any more than by logic: it will come, beyond image and idea, in a mystical state where there is no perception but only the existence of infinite Love.

The title of Forster's novel is apposite. As he says, the passage to *more than* India (to the universal mystical experience which India has made central to its culture) is not easy, not now, not here and not to be apprehended except when it is unattainable. Plotinus also says that to grasp the nature of Unity is not easy but that we have a way through the Ideas. He suggests further that the difficulty for the soul is that the nature of what it is trying to grasp (the Formless) and its means of grasping it (assimilation to it by means of identity) preclude knowledge of attainment. If the passage is not to be apprehended except when it is unattainable, neither is it to be attained except when it is inapprehensible (*Enneads*, VI.ix.3–4; *PI*, xxxvi, 309).[36] At best the novel can operate only at the level of Ideas, of the Imagination. The closest it could come to indicating the abstract mystical state which is said to contain the secret of the earth and sky would be to show an enlightened mind at the level equivalent to its own capacity – that where images are indivisible but multiple – and to depict all the disparate images in the novel in terms of that mind.

A Passage to India does precisely this and on account of it we may argue that Forster is not being sceptical of the Neo-Platonist position but entirely consistent with it when, like Plotinus (*Enneads*, IV.iv.6), he says that it is impossible to tell whether the mystic Vision has succeeded. Language forces him, no less than Plotinus, to resort to the terminology of negation and it is hardly surprising that idealism so refined as to use language identical with that used by materialism should frequently be mistaken for scepticism. What distinguishes it is its aspiration – the negation is that of infinite possibility – and all an idealistic Forster can properly do is portray an India aspirant to something more than India. Forster himself made the nice distinction that his novel *desired to be* – rather than *was* – philosophic and poetic (*PI*, Introduction, p. 25), and the real irony (and glory) of literature is that the aspiration itself may be the infinite dimension to which it aspires.

This reading of the novel suggests that it is not essentially the study of personal or even interracial relationships it is sometimes taken to be but the study of an Impersonalism which reaches out into the common ground not merely of humanity but of existence. There is some reason for regarding *A Passage to India* as one of those imaginative achievements in the Romantic tradition in which Forster, like the Socrates of the *Phaedrus* (247c), surpassed himself in approaching that region about which no earthly poet has yet sung but which even Fielding thinks the Hindus have perhaps found (*PI*, xxxi, 274). The best English Romantic poems may be most fruitfully read not as exercises in egotistical sublimity but as visions of those objective truths which lie in the Imagination, or (in modernised Neo-Platonist parlance) the Collective Unconscious. That Forster's India stands as an image for the Imagination is an idea which receives support from both the shape and substance of the literary criticism Forster wrote in the mid 1920s. In the Clark Lectures, again using that antithetical shape which begins with the material and, through a series of negations, moves towards the immaterial, he argues that good fiction, though perhaps the wrong medium compared with poetry, aspires to the condition of music. Only by touching a mystical region (again rather antithetical to it) can it hope to release the tremendous current that can suddenly flow and, after the reading of the novel is over, allow every item to lead a larger existence than was possible at the time of reading.[37]

Even more pertinent to *A Passage to India* because almost contemporaneous with it and less diffuse than the lecture is the essay 'Anonymity: An Inquiry' (1925). In it, Forster seems to have taken his lead quite directly from the Romantic poets Coleridge and Shelley, who, like him, were responsive to Neo-Platonism. What he really values in writing, he says, is the power words have not simply to quicken our blood but also to do something else which, if it could be defined, would explain the secret of the universe: namely, create a world more real and solid than daily existence. This world 'created by words exists neither in space nor time though it has semblances of both, it is eternal and indestructible. . . . *We can best define it by negations*. It is not this world, its laws are not the laws of science or logic, its conclusions not those of common sense. And it causes us to suspend our ordinary judgments.'[38] The surface personality of the author who creates such a work is wholly eliminated, as is that of the responsive reader, who is transformed towards the condition of the author. This common ground where they meet is called God by the mystics. Such a vision of literature, I would have thought, is not possible to a man who is sceptical about the passage Godbole makes. If I advocate an identification of Forster with Godbole in particular, it is not because the other characters in *A Passage to India* have no significance – Forster's eye for detail and ear for dialogue would always give them that. But they take on the larger, because coherent, significance they do have only because they are seen in terms of the philosophical spirit Godbole embodies.[39] In their own right they are nothing compared to what Godbole has us see they – and we – potentially are. Forster's Godbole is what Forster says Dostoyevsky's Mitya is: at once the novelist's creation and his prophetic vision (*AN*, vii, 92).[40]

One last point. If Godbole is, as I suggest, a Neo-Platonist sage, what has all this to do with India? It is sometimes suggested that the whole European concern with Orientalism is a form of imperialism, a form of cultural penetration designed to encompass and dominate Asia more skilfully than could an army.[41] Much of this Orientalism has been centred on India and undoubtedly the European conception of India has continued to be strongly determined by the approach taken by Alexander's Greeks.[42] From the Greeks has been derived the view of the Indians as a philosophical people, and, while it might be argued that it has served as a justification for imperialism to conceive of them as contemplative rather than active, this view has more often been fostered by those who were possessed by, rather than by those who possessed, India.

A Passage to India is one such work in this tradition and it is no accident that while composing it Forster referred to his novel as a meditation (Introduction, 16). It is a meditation on the power of meditation. When Plotinus asserts that action is a weakened form of contemplation (*Enneads*, iv.iv.43–4) he is very much in accord with the Indian philosophers who told Alexander that conquest of the world was a poor substitute for conquest of the self. There is no antithesis here, although medieval European

monks thought there was.[43] The contemplative power of
Forster's Hindus is actually more effective on the course of
action than any conceivable action could have been.[44] This gives
the lie to a common European assumption which has led
imperialists as well as Marxists to argue that mysticism works to
augment the political *status quo*. In fact the mystical tradition we
have considered is highly subversive in its conviction that there
is within the compass of our minds nothing which is fixed. *A
Passage to India* is overtly subversive of imperialism, but the
view that Forster is a disillusioned Victorian liberal incapable of
becoming a revolutionary is based on the assumption that the
Imagination is determined by social, political and economic
factors. Forster subscribes to the contrary view of the
Neo-Platonists that any worthwhile social, political and
economic system must be the product of an Imagination that is
not constrained by time and place. Poetry is a call not to political
action but to poetry – that is, to realising man's (and nature's)
potential *per se* and to discovering that the world will be
transformed not by conscious manipulation of externals but by a
systematic rediscovery of the Psyche. This does not involve a
rejection of the phenomenal world but a rejection of it outside
the ability of seeing it aright – that is, as the One World which
the thinking of imperialists and Marxists alike divides.

By this token, it is not Orientalism which is a subtle form of
imperialism but, as the story of the Indian ascetics confronting
Alexander indicates, imperialism which is a misplaced form of
Orientalism or at least of that sort of Orientalism which
conceives of the Orient as adhering to a cosmic view greater than
Orient or Occident. *Kim* (1901), no less than *A Passage to India*,
places British imperialism within the context of the cosmic view
of the Indians, and the fact that Kipling's lama is from Tibet may
remind us that the English conception of the Orient since the
time of the Romantics has largely been determined by the extent
of Indian influence throughout Asia.[45] It is the recurrent sense
that India is an appropriate image for man's potential to
discover the whole world within himself[46] which permitted
Forster to image out the Imagination in terms of the Vedantin
mystic Godbole just as Coleridge did in terms of the Buddhist
initiate Kublai Khan[47] and Shelley in terms of a personified Asia
capable of conjuring up an imageless mystical power in the
Indian mountains.[48] *A Passage to India* is one of those works

which, paradoxically using the East as an image to take us out into the common ground where there is neither East nor West, illustrates how the great republic may be built most effectively and enduringly in the republic of letters.[49]

8   *A Passage to India*, the French New Novel and English Romanticism

JOHN BEER

When I first wrote about *A Passage to India* some years back, I was mainly concerned to trace the continuities within Forster's fiction as a whole and their relationship to some central themes in English romanticism. His interest in the human imagination, with its power to betray those who indulged it too easily and to act as an important guide to the nature of reality in those who knew how to and on what terms to trust it, had emerged for me as an important clue in understanding his achievement as a whole, and I argued that it was still at work within the largely negative vision of his Indian novel, contributing to its unusual shape and organisation.[1] In a more recent essay I have taken a closer look at some romantic images, notably those involving echoes and reflections, which are used in that novel and help suggest the ambiguous status of the individual in the universe.[2] I want now to approach it from a different point of view again, looking primarily at those elements in it which have led critics to acclaim it as one of the first great 'modern' novels. In spite of all that has been written about it in recent years, there has been comparatively little attempt to determine its nature as a body of fiction.

A definitive reading obviously is neither desirable nor possible. In an age when, as Frank Kermode has pointed out, we value works for their hermeneutic versatility,[3] there is a good deal to be said for allowing diversity of interpretations to flourish. Yet it remains a part of the critic's task to indicate important contours in the novel's landscape, to draw attention to points of complexity that might otherwise be missed, and to ask what *kind* of novel we are reading.

If we approach *A Passage to India* in formal terms, with this question in mind, the first and most obvious point that is likely to strike us is that it is a failed detective story. To those familiar with detective fiction, the set-up seems familiar enough: the description of scene and characters, the mysterious and sinister event, and the investigation towards a solution. Yet in these terms we are thwarted: there is no 'solution', and we never know what, if anything, happened in the cave.

To readers of a later time, however, this is not quite the frustrating experience it might have been when the novel was first issued, since we have been made familiar with such a situation by our readings in contemporary fiction and particularly in the French new novel, as practised for example by Robbe-Grillet. In such novels, and their equivalent films, a similar situation is often met with: it is only gradually that the reader comes to see that the expectation of a solution was after all the mark of a false attitude on his part. And even some things which Robbe-Grillet has said about the new novel strike one, at least at first sight, as things that might be said also about *A Passage to India*. He talks, for instance, of a common effect to be found in a thriller:

> the plot starts to thicken alarmingly: witnesses contradict one another, the suspect multiplies his alibis, new factors crop up which had previously been overlooked. . . . And you have to keep coming back to the recorded evidence: the exact position of a piece of furniture, the shape and frequency of a fingerprint, a word written in a message. The impression grows on you that nothing else is *true*. Whether they conceal or reveal a mystery, these elements that defy all systems have only one serious, obvious quality – that of being *there*.[4]

Whether or not that is true of the average thriller, it is true in an important sense of *A Passage*: the existence of the mystery drives us back to a sense less of what might have happened in the Marabar Caves than of the evidence: the smashed binoculars, Adela Quested's shock and above all the caves themselves, described as exactly as possible by the author and presented as preceding by thousands of years not only the petty fates of individual human beings but the human race itself.

Robbe-Grillet goes on to describe the traditional forms of narrative – 'the systematic use of the past definite tense and of the third person, the unconditional adoption of chronological development, linear plots, a regular graph of the emotions, the way each episode tended towards an end, etc.' – and sees them as all having been devoted to the imposition of 'the image of a stable universe, coherent, continuous, univocal and wholly decipherable', commenting that 'as the intelligibility of the world was never even questioned, the act of narration raised no problems'.

When we recall a later comment of Forster's on his novel, 'I tried to indicate the human predicament in a universe which is not, so far, comprehensible to our minds', it is not perhaps surprising to discover that the use of the past definite tense and of strict chronological definition is sometimes violated, that the plot though more or less linear leads not to a conclusion but to an uncertainty, and that the picture of the universe is, to adapt Robbe-Grillet's phraseology, incoherent, discontinuous, multi-vocal ('India in her thousand voices') and largely undecipherable.

Again, we might turn to Robbe-Grillet's comments on solitude:

Let us as an example, recapitulate the functioning of 'solitude'. I call. No one answers me. Instead of concluding that there is no one there – which could be an observation, pure and simple, dated and placed, in space and time – I decide to act as if someone were in fact there, and as if, for one reason or another, he were refusing to answer. From then on the silence that follows my appeal is no longer a real silence, it has become pregnant with content, with depth, with a soul – which immediately plunges me back into my own soul. The distance between my cry, as I hear it, and the mute (perhaps deaf) interlocutor to whom it is addressed, becomes a sort of anguish, my hope and my despair, a sense to my life. Henceforth nothing will count for me save this false vacuum and the problems it causes me. Should I go on calling? Should I call more loudly? Should I use other words? I try again. . . . I very soon realise that no one is going to answer, but the invisible presence that I continue to create by my cry forces me to go on, for all eternity, sending out my unhappy cry into the silence. Its echo soon starts to deafen me.[5]

It is hard to read these words without recalling the well-known passage in which Forster describes the effect upon Mrs Moore's consciousness of the echo she had heard in the Marabar cave:

The crush and the smells she could forget, but the echo began in some indescribable way to undermine her hold on life. Coming at a moment when she chanced to be fatigued, it had managed to murmur: 'Pathos, piety, courage – they exist, but are identical, and so is filth. Everything exists, nothing has value.' If one had spoken vileness in that place, or quoted lofty poetry, the comment would have been the same – 'ou-boum'. If one had spoken with the tongues of angels and pleaded for all the unhappiness and misunderstanding in the world, past, present, and to come, for all the misery men must undergo whatever their opinion and position, and however much they dodge or bluff – it would amount to the same, the serpent would descend and return to the ceiling. (*PI*, xv, 160–1)

This effect is reinforced when we turn back to the original manuscript and discover that in that version, in which a physical attack on Adela is described, she found her cries for help met simply by the Marabar echo; we also learn that the passage about the power of the echo to negate values was at first associated with Fielding – and that Fielding actually went into a cave and started declaiming noble and resonant poetry (the opening of *Paradise Lost*, a poem by Meredith, a Persian poem taught him by Aziz), only to find each greeted and replied to by the same dull noise.[6] In the final version Forster simply made this scene a *possibility*, to be contemplated by Mrs Moore's (or perhaps merely the reader's) consciousness, but it remains one of the key statements in the novel. Although we cannot ignore the difference in what Robbe-Grillet is saying (in his novel it is the silence that echoes, not a cave) we recognise a common predicament.

Perhaps the most striking point of correspondence between Robbe-Grillet's novels and *A Passage to India*, however, lies in a common feature of their construction as a whole. Some

commentators (including Robbe-Grillet himself) have noted
that there is in most of his novels an important gap at the heart of
what is going on. In terms of the plot it is often no more than a
gap in the chronology of events, but it may also be given a visual
correlative. Roger Sturrock has discussed some of these: in *Les
Gommes*, there is a gap between the drawbridge and the road as
the drawbridge finally settles, quaveringly, into position, and
the impossibility of being certain just when there is a gap and
when there is not emphasises the precarious condition of all
perceptual interpretations of events. In *La Maison de Rendez-
vous*, more strikingly, the events take place in a restaurant
anchored in the harbour (and so surrounded by water) in the
middle of which there is a hole, a square pool in whose green
water may be seen 'a multitude of huge fish, blue, violet, red or
yellow'. Sturrock argues that this pool corresponds to the gap at
the centre of the narrative which gives the fantasies of his
characters space to breed.[7]

Encounter with such a gap, a gap which cannot be controlled,
induces a situation in which the very thing that is not there can
assume a size out of all proportion to its own significance – what
Robbe-Grillet himself calls 'the void which overruns, which fills
everything'.[8] We may compare Adela Quested's reaction to the
echo:

> the noise in the cave, so unimportant intellectually, was
> prolonged over the surface of her life. . . . The sound had
> spouted after her when she escaped, and was going on still like
> a river that gradually fills the plain. Only Mrs Moore could
> drive it back to its source and seal the broken reservoir.   (*PI*,
> xxii, 200)

Adela Quested also manifests something which one recognises
from Robbe-Grillet's novels: the tendency of those who have
become aware of such a void or gap to indulge in obsessive
activity. While the cactus spines are being plucked from her
body she is haunted by the phrase, 'In space things touch, in time
things part' (184), which she repeats over and over again,
uncertain whether it is a philosophy or a pun. It is neither,
perhaps, but it does remind us of something that Blake also
wrote about: the tendency of the mind that has become aware of

an uninterpretable void to concentrate on finding a firm point of
organisation, if possible in terms of space and time.[9]

Adela Quested's obsessive activity transcends the kind
described by Robbe-Grillet or Blake, however, since she retains
awareness of the problem that she is facing. Rather, the activity
of her mind is a circular process, first wrestling honestly with the
problem and then being overtaken for a time by the irrational
powers of her personality:

> Adela was always trying to 'think the incident out', always
> reminding herself that no harm had been done. There was 'the
> shock', but what is that? For a time her own logic would
> convince her, then she would hear the echo again, weep,
> declare she was unworthy of Ronny, and hope her assailant
> would get the maximum penalty. After one of these bouts, she
> longed to go out into the bazaars and ask pardon from
> everyone she met, for she felt in some vague way that she was
> leaving the world worse than she found it. She felt that it was
> her crime, until the intellect, reawakening, pointed out to her
> that she was inaccurate here, and set her again upon her
> sterile round.   (p. 200)

We recall Blake again:

> If it were not for the Poetic or Prophetic character the
> Philosophic & Experimental would soon be at the ratio of all
> things, & stand still, unable to do other than repeat the same
> dull round over again.[10]

Adela Quested attains the 'Poetic or Prophetic character' only
once in the novel, however, in the court room; and then the
pressure of the context is such that her poetic and prophetic
utterance can articulate itself only in the statement 'I am not
quite sure' (xxiv, 231).

This kind of obsessive activity in Adela's mind is richer and
more complex than that of Robbe-Grillet's characters, where
the obsessive activity is more strictly cerebral, falling back upon
some simple inviolable order. I am thinking for instance of the
husband in *La Jalousie* who occupies himself in counting and
organising in his mind the banana trees on his plantation, only to
find that the pattern will never quite come together; or still more

closely the bicyclist salesman in *Le Voyeur* who occupies himself in calculating how long he can devote to selling each of his watches if he is to sell eighty-nine during the time he has to spend on the island, only to be seized by panic when talking to a boy who he thinks may have seen him assaulting a young girl:

> He began to talk at such a rate that objections – or regret at his own words – became quite impossible. In order to fill in the gaps he often repeated the same sentence several times. He even surprised himself reciting the multiplication table.[11]

This kind of activity seems to be paralleled in Forster's novel rather by the behaviour of Mrs Moore after the visit to the caves. Her speech, it will be remembered, becomes highly repetitive:

> 'all this rubbish about love, love in a church, love in a cave, as if there is the least difference, and I held up from my business over such trifles!'
> 'What do you want?' he said, exasperated. 'Can you state it in simple language? If so, do.'
> 'I want my pack of patience cards.'   (xxii, 207)

And so Mrs Moore sidesteps any possibility of facing the unfaceable by retreating to the strictly organised code of a solitary card game, played over and over again, obsessively. And yet in her presence, Adela becomes convinced that Mrs Moore has in some way proclaimed Aziz's innocence – so much so that Ronny in the end asks her.

> She replied: 'I never said his name', and began to play patience.
> 'I thought you said, "Aziz is an innocent man", but it was in Mr Fielding's letter.'
> 'Of course he is innocent', she answered indifferently; it was the first time she had expressed an opinion on the point.
> 'You see, Ronny, I was right', said the girl.
> 'You were not right, she never said it.'
> 'But she thinks it.'
> 'Who cares what she thinks?'
> 'Red nine on black ten –' from the card-table.   (p. 209)

When the others force her back into conversation her talk becomes apparently irrelevant, rambling and repetitive; but when Adela asks if the case cannot now be withdrawn, and is told by Ronny 'the case has to come before a magistrate now; it really must, the machinery has started', Mrs Moore chips in with

'She has started the machinery; it will work to its end.'

It is at this moment that Ronny decides that she ought to leave India: 'she was doing no good to herself or to anyone else there' (p. 211).

So far it might seem that the drift of the argument is pushing *A Passage to India* more and more into the role of precursor to the new novel, as it has emerged in France since the Second World War. It is time to point out some differences. It shares with them a defeat of the normal expectation that a plot will end in some clear resolution; it also shares a tendency (associated with the first, perhaps) to bring into question the whole process of fiction itself. We might, for instance, consider the opening to chapter xiv of Forster's novel:

Most of life is so dull that there is nothing to be said about it, and the books and talk that would describe it as interesting are obliged to exaggerate, in the hope of justifying their own existence.   (p. 145)

In such a statement Forster might seem to be aligning himself with those novelists who have argued for the total deconstruction of plot on the grounds that plot does violence to the unorganised, plotless nature of most human experience.

Yet of course Forster deconstructs his plot a good deal less than he would if he were pursuing the implications of that remark in any determined manner. Whereas in the *nouveau roman* we are left in serious doubt as to what has been happening – and in some cases whether anything at all has happened throughout the plot – Forster localises such uncertainties to one place and one time. One might indeed wonder whether there is any uncertainty at all, particularly when it is discovered that in the manuscript version Adela Quested *was* assaulted physically. Yet, if we stick to the final text and that alone, the uncertainty is clearly there, and we know that Forster meant it to be there, from an important letter which he wrote to Lowes Dickinson shortly after the novel appeared. Even here, however, it will be noticed that he is concerned to limit the range of possibilities quite strictly to three, instead of allowing them to proliferate as a later novelist might. Dickinson had asked what had happened in the cave. Forster replied,

> In the cave it is *either* a man, *or* the supernatural, *or* an illusion. If I say, it becomes whatever the answer a different book. And even if I know! My writing mind therefore is a blur here – i.e. I will it to remain a blur, and to be uncertain, as I am of many facts in daily life. This isn't a philosophy of aesthetics. *It's a particular trick I felt justified in trying because my theme was India*. It sprang straight from my subject matter. I wouldn't have attempted it in other countries, which though they contain mysteries or muddles, manage to draw rings round them. Without the trick I doubt whether I could have got the spiritual reverberation going. I call it 'trick': but 'voluntary surrender to infection' better expresses my state.[12]

This letter is important not only because it seems to settle, once and for all, what Forster's own view of the event, or non-event, in the cave was; it also openly disavows any deliberate generalising intent. His creative posture, he implies, was passive: he adopted this course because his subject was India, and this uncertainty suited it, was to some extent forced upon him by it.

This very limited disorganisation of plot is matched by an equally limited disruption of chronology. So far as chronology within the plot structure is concerned, there are no problems: everything seems to fit neatly and exactly. But if we begin to ask just when the events of the novel as a whole took place, it is not altogether easy to be sure. Some details of the novel, like the Lieutenant-Governor and the dogcarts, belong to an earlier period, while references to the Amritsar massacre place the timing of the novel as contemporary with its first publication. Yet again we suddenly find Forster saying in chapter xxix that, after Aziz had generously renounced his claim for compensation,

> it won him no credit with the English. They still believed he

was guilty, they believed it to the end of their careers, and retired Anglo-Indians in Tunbridge Wells or Cheltenham still murmur to each other: 'That Marabar case which broke down because the poor girl couldn't face giving her evidence – that was another bad case.'   (p. 259)

If we adopt the time scale presupposed by that remark, we find ourselves suddenly transported to a vantage point in, say, the 1960s. But such literal-mindedness would be out of place; it would be truer to say that we are being invited to view the events from an Olympian standpoint which takes us out of time altogether, while at the same time suggesting that we are dealing with permanent human obtusenesses.

Another place in the novel where the sense of time is noticeably affected has something of the same quality. It is the beginning of the 'Temple' section, where Forster originally wrote as his opening sentence,

Some hundreds of miles westward of the Marabar Hills, and two years later in time, Professor Narayan Godbole stood in the presence of God.[13]

He then changed 'stood' to 'stands', and goes on to take us out of time in the next sentence as well: 'God is not born yet . . . but He has also been born centuries ago, nor can He ever be born, because He is the Lord of the Universe. . . . He is, was not, is not, was' (xxxiii, 281).

It is in this extension of the Olympian attitude to time that we begin to discover another important difference between Forster's novel and the new novel of Robbe-Grillet and others which can be traced also in their relative attitudes to mythology.

Some critics have found a 'mythological' element in Robbe-Grillet's novels; in such cases they are read as presentations of Freudian mythology, with its strangely self-destructive quality. By this I mean that the most dominant myths of Freud's writing, such as the myth of Oedipus, have a powerful and even looming presence there; yet in the end the logic of the argument would seem to turn back on the myths themselves, to see them, too, as projections of human needs and desires. They do not have the authority of myths that are presented as having a more general or objective status. And Robbe-Grillet's novels present Oedipal imagery with a certain priority, but without allowing the reader to accord them more than a provisional status. Their status, in other words, refers them back to the individual human being, and Oedipus remains a riddle. Even in the work of a novelist such as Michel Butor, who gives mythology more play, there are limitations: a myth is defined as 'a form of social hygiene' and the need for it is seen as a bulwark against the dissolution of society that must otherwise come about; it is seen as essentially something that we make up ourselves and for particular purposes.

Forster's approach, by contrast, gives mythology a greater life of its own. He allows for a possible metaphysical validity of myth in a way that psychoanalytic accounts, at least of the Freudian kind, normally do not. And at this point it is profitable to turn to another of Forster's accounts of his novel, given some thirty or so years later in a talk entitled 'Three Countries'. Here, as in the programme note quoted from earlier, he acknowledges the political significance of his novel, but also draws attention to further elements in it which transcend local questions:

> the book is not really about politics, though it is the political aspect of it that caught the general public and made it sell. It's about something wider than politics, about the search of the human race for a more lasting home, about the universe as embodied in the Indian earth and the Indian sky, about the horror lurking in the Marabar Caves and the release symbolized by the birth of Krishna. It is – or rather desires to be – philosophic and poetic. (*HD*, pp. 289–99)

When Forster says that the novel is about the search of the human race for a more lasting home, about the universe as embodied in the Indian earth and the Indian sky, and the horror lurking in the Marabar Caves, we can recognise elements which might well make up a *nouveau roman*. But when he speaks of a release, 'symbolized by the birth of Krishna', it is harder to see any correlative in that kind of novel. Release is precisely what seems often to be lacking. And it is Forster's willingness to allow the Hindu element in his novel to flourish so fully that gives a quite different kind of shape to his conclusion. The reader feels that the Hindu values are hovering on the point of being accepted and affirmed by the novelist himself. 'No man could say where was the emotional centre' of the Hindu festival, 'any more than he could locate the heart of a cloud' – but it is hard to resist the sense that it had one, all the same.

The novel can be read in orthodox Hindu terms with some fidelity. On this reading of the novel, the British characters find the caves horrifying simply because they have not been initiated into the larger sense of the universe that a fuller acquaintance with Hinduism would have given them.

For a Hindu the cave would not be horrifying: it would rather be the retiring-place of the individual which he enters in order to commune with God. The Barabar Caves which Forster visited were not, like the Marabar Caves of his novel, untouched by human hand; they had served as monastic cells for those who wished to meditate alone and were, as he later acknowledged in his notes, ornamented. Several writers have pointed out, similarly, that the pronouncing and meditating upon the syllable 'ОМ' is part of the meditative discipline in certain forms of Indian religion, so that even the sinister 'ou-boum or bou-oum' could for such a meditator become simply a natural echo of his own deepest meditations, a reverberation of 'ОМ'.[14]

At the same time this seems to be a set of significances that exist outside the novel rather than within the text that is presented to us. Forster later described his own delight on discovering that the symbolism of the Hindu temple was that of a world mountain enclosing a central cavern where the individual could be alone with his god, but that was evidently a subsequent recognition.[15] The British in this novel are caught rather (as perhaps he himself was at the time) between the decline of their own religion and a failure to apprehend any other. The religious associations of the caves are deliberately eliminated by Forster; equally deliberately he sets his characters in a place which is, in its essence, older than any human religion.

Some critics, pursuing a different line of thought, have noted the physiological reference of the 'fists and fingers' and seized upon the possible interpretation of the caves as wombs. The point finds natural support in Freudian analysis and has been developed by Wilfred Stone in a memorable discussion which quotes among other things Norman Douglas on cave worship as the cult of the feminine principle.[16] At the same time I have come across no source in Hindu thought which would ascribe such meaning to the cave, and it is noticeable that this is a significance that Forster himself never suggests in his imagery. What he does say many years later in looking back at the planning of the incident is that the caves 'were something to focus everything up; they were to engender an event like an egg'.[17] And in a later incident of the novel, it will be remembered, Aziz, looking to see the cave into which Adela has disappeared, finds that 'Caves appeared in every direction – it seemed their original spawning-place . . .' (*PI*, xvi, 265). Forster once again delicately balances disgust and delight in fecundity by that word 'spawning'; but as soon as one focuses more sharply on the image one sees that, while caves which spawn may be eggs, they are also, by definition, hollow eggs.

My point here is not to discount either Hindu or Freudian interpretations of the novel, but to suggest that they hardly have Forster's own authority behind them: they are significances which one may discover in the novel, just as one may discover them in Forster's own personality, but which he himself would seem to be excluding – perhaps deliberately. His various descriptions of the caves combine to resist any identification of them with the womb – at least if that is thought of as a source of warmth and life. Rather, they focus his questionings of the significance of the universe, once there is removed from it the normal pattern of birth, generation and death by which most human beings live, and it is an essential feature of that questioning that it should resist the imposition of any significance derived from a traditional religion.

Nothing I have said, obviously, is intended to derogate from the centrality of the cave imagery in the novel: on the contrary it needs to be examined with extreme care. The need for vigilance is intensified, moreover, by Forster's refusal (a refusal which, it will be recalled, Dr Leavis found disturbing[18]) to write to a consistent degree of seriousness or to signal clearly his transitions from whimsy to something more ambiguous. In this context it is useful to recall one of Furbank's observations on Forster: that he had a habit of realising images with an unexpected literalness. On one occasion, for instance, he described how he had, like a rat, deserted the sinking ship of fiction, 'and *swam* towards biography'. Or again, when a friend said to him 'One must face facts', he replied, 'How can I, when they're all about me?'[19] When he opens his chapter on the Marabar Caves with the words, 'The Ganges, though flowing from the foot of Vishnu and through Siva's hair, is not an ancient stream', we are tempted to read the statement in much the same way that we read his joke in the first chapter: 'There are no bathing-steps on the river-front, as the Ganges happens not to be holy here.' If so, we may still not take him very seriously when a few lines later we find him saying of the caves themselves,

> They are older than anything in the world. No water has ever covered them, and the sun who has watched them for countless aeons may still discern in their outlines forms that were his before our globe was torn from his bosom . . . (xii, 137)

Further attention to the image, allowing the sentence to resonate in its own right, causes a quite different vision to emerge – particularly when Forster continues, 'If flesh of the sun's flesh is to be touched anywhere, it is here, among the incredible antiquity of these hills'. For in what sense can either the caves, or at the opposite extreme the sun, be thought of as having *flesh*? Realise the image and you are left with a stark dialectic: an eye of everlasting life gazing at the dead flesh of its own body. The idea can temporarily take over and interpret the whole universe: we recognise that all human beings are in moments of starker awareness eyes of everlasting life which are forced to contemplate the necessary death of their own flesh.

Close attention of this kind, involving expansive interpretation, is further justified by evidences of calculation in Forster's handling of his material. We have already noted that the Barabar Caves of actuality had different kinds of entrance, some simple squares, others elaborately ornamented, each showing strong human influence; the Marabar Caves, by contrast, are described as all alike and apparently untouched by human art. Forster suggests also that there are a great number of them – and still more perhaps which have no entrance from the outside world; at the Barabar Caves there were only seven, and none at all at the Kawa Dol, the place where they are actually visited in the novel (*PI*, Notes, pp. 347–8). In an author who tries where possible to be precise and factual, this emphasis on the non-human is likely to be a calculated effect.

Close reading at this point in the novel also reveals an 'echoing' effect in the use of certain keywords. That is, the word or phrase will impress itself upon the mind in one way, but then, attended to again will reveal another meaning, and then perhaps another. The word 'extraordinary', read first in its normal sense of 'out of the ordinary', can return to the eye in the sense of '*extra* ordinary' – that is, even more ordinary than usual; and then again simply as extra, ordinary – that is, no more than a simple addition to the sum of ordinary events. The visitor returns from the Marabar Caves, says Forster, uncertain whether he has had an interesting experience, or a dull one or no experience at all. He does not know, in other words, whether what he found there was extraordinary, *extra* ordinary or just extra, and ordinary.

This is not, perhaps, a kind of reading commonly called for in Forster's writings. It is invited in this novel, however, and at this point of the novel, by the very way in which the author himself refers to his key word:

> It is as if the surrounding plain or the passing birds have taken upon themselves to exclaim "Extraordinary!" and the word has taken root in the air, and been inhaled by mankind.   (xii, 138)

A word that can behave like that is clearly to be looked at with some care. Another, more complicated example of a phrase echoing in the mind to reveal different layers of significance comes in the description of that archetypal Marabar cave, the one supposed to subsist within the hollow boulder of the Kawa Dol that sways in the wind:

> a bubble-shaped cave that has neither ceiling nor floor, and mirrors its own darkness in every direction infinitely. If the boulder falls and smashes, the cave will smash too – empty as an Easter egg.   (p. 139)

On its first impact that smashing has a rather appalling effect, since a void which had at least possessed form is suddenly transformed into utter non-existence. Yet the image of the Easter egg, on the echo, limits the feeling of appalledness by domesticating it. We are reminded rather of the disappointment of a child at discovering that the marvellous looking egg turns out to have nothing but hollowness inside it – a sharp disappointment for the moment, perhaps, but one that is quickly mitigated by the pieces of chocolate that remain. No sooner has that softening of the blow been registered, on the other hand, than a third echo of the phrase brings us up against the word Easter and reminds us that *this* Easter egg is an empty cave. We are reminded of the empty cave that might transform human experience by realising an unthinkable possibility of resurrection but is more likely to confirm humanity in its own scepticism. The swaying of the boulder itself emphasises, meanwhile, the instability and fragility of human conceptions of the universe and man's place in it.

A striking feature of Forster's description of the caves is his use of images that bring out different possible significances but also fall away from one another, so thwarting any one overall pattern of interpretation. Take, for instance, the first approach to the caves, which comes after the small *contretemps* between Adela and Dr Aziz. The slight coldness that has overtaken their relationship is registered in a single, formal Jane Austen-like sentence: 'The first cave was tolerably convenient.' Then

> The small black hole gaped where their varied forms and colours had momentarily functioned. They were sucked in like water down a drain.

Following this the scene without humanity is described – the scene as it must always have looked – after which we read

> And then the hole belched, and humanity returned. (xiv, 158)

The hole which a moment ago was like a drain, so connecting with an imagery of excretory functions, has turned into a rejecting mouth – but humanity is not spewed forth, it is belched forth. The suggestion that has emerged is of silent water disappearing down a drain – which comes back now as noise in the belching.

Other ambiguities, which are actually dramatised in the text, respect this duality of invited response. As elephants take the party up to the Marabar Hills, for example, mounds are seen by the track which might be either graves or breasts of the goddess

Parvati (the villagers give both explanations); these alternative explanations of death or superfecundity then modulate into something doubly sinister when Adela Quested sees a thin dark object which she identifies as a snake, only to see through her field glasses that it is the withered and twisted stump of a toddy palm. The alternative here is between the deadly and the deathly – and the fact that the villagers continue to insist that it is a snake now that the idea is in their heads merely assists the underlying sense of hollowness and nullity which is already there in the spiritual silence of the journey, where 'sounds did not echo or thoughts develop' (p. 152). It is as if the villagers are wantonly superimposing interpretation upon a void.

This underlying, further sense is reinforced by the increasing use of an imagery which is on the point of becoming uninterpretable, such as the drain imagery cited above, or that of caves which are 'spawned' yet have 'orifices'. It reaches its apogee, perhaps, in the moment when Aziz realises that it is of no use to shout, 'because a Marabar cave can hear no sound but its own' (xvi, 165). Robbe-Grillet's account of 'solitude' is marvellously caught, and extended, here.

I have spoken up to now as if the ambiguities of the experience in the cave normally showed a bias either towards the sinister or at least the life-denying, and that is no doubt true of the novel's main effect. There is however one indication of positive value in the caves which is not checked or negated anywhere else, though by the end of the paragraph its effect has been carefully restricted. I am thinking of the moment when a visitor strikes a match in the cave:

Immediately another flame rises in the depths of the rock and moves towards the surface like an imprisoned spirit; the walls of the circular chamber have been most marvellously polished. The two flames approach and strive to unite, but cannot, because one of them breathes air, the other stone. A mirror inlaid with lovely colours divides the lovers, delicate stars of pink and gray interpose, exquisite nebulae, shadings fainter than the tail of a comet or the midday moon, all the evanescent life of the granite, only here visible. Fists and fingers thrust above the advancing soil – here at last is their skin, finer than any covering acquired by the animals, smoother than windless water, more voluptuous than love.

> The radiance increases, the flames touch one another, kiss, expire. The cave is dark again, like all the caves.   (xii, 138–9)

The final emphasis, as so often in this novel, is upon limitation. The flames can never unite; the power of physical surface intervenes; light is surrounded by, and yields to, darkness. Yet that need not close the reader's eyes to what has opened out in the course of the paragraph. It is only under the rules of time which govern sequential fiction that the darkness triumphs; in another sense the beauty, inherent in the very rock itself, has opened another dimension. It has intimated the possible existence of a timeless order which might have an eternal value, and so gestured towards an absolute romanticism.

This theme in the novel is reflected in the aftermath of Mrs Moore's collapse. Even as she falls under the rules of time and yields to the limitations of her body her spirit remains alive in a strange, disembodied manner. Even while she is talking on repetitively in her weary, irritable voice, Adela hears her as declaring Aziz's innocence; and, even when she is dead, there continues in the chant of the crowd outside the court room, and in the remembering consciousness of her friends, a sense of connection – that 'connection' which is of chief importance to Forster and which is for him one of the mysteries in a nature whose mechanical processes might otherwise seem to confirm the existence of impenetrable surfaces between individuals.

What is no more than a hint with Mrs Moore, moreover, becomes actual momentarily, in Adela, in her experience in the court room, where the whole baffling experience of the caves is seen by her transformed into unity, and even as splendid.

> Why had she thought the expedition 'dull'? Now the sun rose again, the elephant waited, the pale masses of the rock flowed round her and presented the first cave . . .   (xxiv, 230)

The effect of this passage, like that of some words discussed earlier, depends on the reader's willingness or otherwise to change his mode of reading. Cast into sequence it is quickly lost in the flow of the events of the court room; lingered on and contemplated, it offers the hint of a different psychic order, an alternative vision of humanity which might stand in judgement on time's processes just as the naked punkah wallah who rouses

Adela from her state of unreality stands in separation from all that is going on in the court room.

The existence of such passages and images throughout the novel is the mark of a persistent trait in Forster, a willingness to be sceptical about his own scepticism and to acknowledge the existence of a possible metaphysical dimension in human experience which is accepted and acknowledged by the human imagination itself under certain conditions.

It is here that his debt to the early Romantics is most evident. In his essay 'My Own Centenary' (*AH*, pp. 59–61), Forster drew upon the coincidence that the centenaries of Beethoven and Blake both fell in the year in which he was writing (1927) to project a sermon in 2027 by the Dean of Dulborough which would compare him with those two predecessors. The self-effacing irony of that comparison, emphasised by the Dean's platitudes, swings upon its axis to reveal a further depth when one recalls their importance as presences in his own art. His devotion to Beethoven, which he never lost, was evidenced memorably in *Howards End*; it was to him that he owed some of the continuing energy and explorative impulses in his work as a whole. But it is Blake, perhaps, who is a better guide to the mazes of *A Passage to India*. We have argued that Forster's novel is characterised by moments of transforming imagination, such as Adela's experience in the court room, which the reader is invited to set outside the narrative of the novel, in interpretative transcendence. The novel works to its fullest effect for readers who are willing to allow themselves this degree of flexibility and for such a reading one can think of no better preparation than an acquaintance with Blake. Forster's own attitude to him was best indicated, perhaps, in a review of his poems which began 'Blake is a man whom one is ashamed to review. One's feelings lie deep and are vague. . . .'[20] He was forced to be 'vague' since he could not altogether endorse Blake's commitment to the imagination, however much he might admire it; the 'depth' of feeling referred to was based both on a respect for Blake the individual and on an unusually good grasp of Blake's philosophy – which may well have been reflected in detail in the novel. When he describes Aziz cycling through the 'arid tidiness' of the British houses in Chandrapore, he also comments,

> The roads, named after victorious generals and intersecting at
> right angles, were symbolic of the net Great Britain had
> thrown over India.   (ii, 39)

Blake had used his image of the net of Urizen in precisely the
same way: Urizen imposed a mathematical grid over the
universe which then turned into a net in which humanity
struggled. There is even an illustration in the *Songs of Innocence
and Experience* which shows the process in action.[21] The British
Raj, on this reading, takes on the attributes of an obsessive work
of self-confirmation, undertaken by an occupying power whose
philosophy is blinkered by a narrow nationalism.

The suspicion that Forster is drawing on Blake's philosophy
here to suggest the precarious foundations of the British attitude
(strong, like Urizen's, in the short term but constructed
ultimately upon a conception of human nature which must end
in despair), finds support in the review just referred to, where he
goes on to say of Blake,

> To handle him from the outside is to fall into the error of his
> demiurge Urizen, who withdrew from the primal unity, and,
> applying laws to the universe, brought everything, himself
> included, to destruction. Urizen saw that his rule was wrong,
> he 'wept and called it pity', but, entangled in chains meant for
> others, he supposed that the alternative to law is lawlessness,
> he could not imagine the service of perfect freedom.

Forster's conception of what that service might be like was
nourished by a sharp sense, derived from the Romantic poets
generally, of the energies and illuminations which enabled
human beings to signal to one another across the barriers that
divided them. The overall tone of his later works would be one
of kindly scepticism, but it would be accompanied by many
touches which transcend that scepticism and which derived from
what he had learnt in his earlier creative achievement. The
duality of vision which had not only survived but had even been
strengthened by his encounter with India gave him, in fact, both
an unusual insight into the nature of individual freedom and a
tenacious energy in serving it.

It is at such points that Forster's purposes diverge most
radically from those of the new novelists. To believe that the

human heart can find any valid response in nature, or that the imagination can enjoy privileged knowledge would be beyond the terms of their presuppositions. Yet the divergence is not quite so deep as one might think, since by very reason of being creative writers they all share the kind of knowledge that can come from practice of the novelist's art. In *The Hill of Devi*, Forster tells how he took his unfinished Indian chapters to India with him in 1921, hoping that renewal of the experience would help set the novel in motion again. On the contrary,

> as soon as they were confronted with the country they purported to describe, they seemed to wilt and go dead and I could do nothing with them. I used to look at them of an evening in my room in Dewas, and felt only distaste and despair. The gap between India remembered and India experienced was too wide.   (p. 99)

There is something very like this in Robbe-Grillet's description of how, when he was writing *Le Voyeur*, as he was trying to describe in detail the flight of seagulls and the movement of waves, he made a brief trip to the Brittany coast:

> On my way there I said to myself: this is a good opportunity to observe things 'from life' and to 'refresh my memory' . . . . But the moment I saw my first sea bird I realised how wrong I had been: on the one hand the seagulls I was now seeing had only the vaguest connection with the ones I was describing in my book, and on the other hand I was quite indifferent to this fact. The only seagulls that mattered to me at that moment were the ones in my mind. They too had probably come, in one way or another, from the external world, and perhaps even from Brittany, but they had been transformed, and at the same time had seemed to become more real, *because* they were now imaginary.[22]

Robbe-Grillet's statement suggests that he is acknowledging the right of imagination to its own autonomous play. It is an acknowledgement which bears not only on the novelist's art, but also on that of the reader, who thus turns out to be making contact, not primarily with an objective reality, but with the novelist's imagination.

It can indeed be argued that such a novelist's very negations and denials set up conditions of imaginative freedom for the reader. One is reminded of Keats's comment on the lack of precise detail in Milton's description of Pandaemonium:

> What creates the intense pleasure of not knowing? A sense of independence, of power, from the fancy's creating a world of its own by the sense of probabilities.[23]

The statement looks forward to much in modern fiction, where novelists have learned to exploit the 'intense pleasure of not knowing'. It also suggests ways in which the new novel, despite an apparent bias towards determinism, serves the cause of individual freedom.

Forster's own passage to freedom took him by a different route. In so far as he could find a firm historical tradition for his belief in the value of the imagination it would have been the Platonism of his friend Lowes Dickinson. Lowes Dickinson however, who accompanied him on his first visit to India, found his sense of values stifled and oppressed by what he found there: 'I remember how he used to cower away from those huge architectural masses, those pullulating forms, as if a wind blew off them which might wither the soul.'[24] At that level, Forster evidently shared his reaction to some degree. It is not only enacted dramatically in Mrs Moore's collapse but also acknowledged even in his Indian characters. By comparison with the real-life Rabindranath Tagore, who had written (in a poem published the year Forster visited India for the first time), 'Many a song have I sung in many a mood of mind, but all their notes have always proclaimed, "He comes, comes, ever comes" ',[25] Forster's Godbole is less positive:

> 'I say to Shri Krishna, "Come! Come to me only". The God refuses to come . . . .'
> 'But He comes in some other song, I hope?' said Mrs Moore gently.
> 'Oh no, he refuses to come. . . . I say to Him, "Come, come, come, come, come, come." He neglects to come.' (vii, 96)

Godbole's rueful yet accepting avowal presents yet another

response to the conflict between imaginative affirmation and sceptical recognition which is central to this novel. Forster's own solution, as we have traced it, takes two forms. Against the despair induced by the recognition that 'in India nothing is identifiable' or that 'nothing comprehends the whole of India, nothing, nothing' he would set the recognition, carried over from *Howards End*, that 'it is private life that holds out the mirror to infinity; personal intercourse, and that alone, that ever hints at a personality beyond our daily vision' (x, 79). Mrs Moore's survival in the consciousness of others reaffirms his belief in the magic of personal relationships; but it needs for its full effect to be reinforced by the other hints of a link between 'infinity' and 'the personality beyond our daily vision' that are inherent in the descriptions of beauty and culminate perhaps in Adela's court room vision.

We have also seen, however, how the structure of the novel works to enclose that vision, imposing the language and imagery of limitation so strongly that a conventional reading of the narrative might end with a conviction that they had been finally negated. The very instabilities in the novel help focus the reader's attention upon that which does not change, upon the resistancies of things. The sense of inevitable separateness which is induced by the caves is given further point by the failure of the flames to cross the polished barrier that reflects them and (most memorably) by the rocks that the earth sends up in the last sentence of the novel to force riders into single file.

In these respects, Forster's novel foreshadows effects which are later to be made central to the new novel. Robbe-Grillet, indeed, sees their development as the only possible way forward for fiction, as several of his own statements testify:

> In the construction of future novels, gestures and objects will be *there*, before they are *something*; and they will still be there afterwards, hard, unalterable, ever-present, and apparently quite indifferent to their own meaning. . . .
> But from now on . . . objects will gradually lose their instability and their secrets, they will forego their false mystery. . . .
> the future hero will on the contrary remain *there* . . . .[26]

The rhetoric of such expressions is such as to suggest a finality in these new perceptions, a final arrival at the truth of things, uncluttered by the affections or the search for ultimate meanings. This is natural enough, since most artists need the security that derives from the sense of driving towards an ultimate truth, a point of achieved precision. Yet there is no logical reason why the assertions that Robbe-Grillet is making must be finally valid for all time; elsewhere, indeed, he acknowledges the danger of predicting the course of fiction too far ahead, emphasising the overall importance of development. 'Form in the novel has to evolve to stay alive', he writes, and 'There is no question . . . of establishing a theory, a pre-cast mould in which to pour the books of the future. All novelists, and all novels, must invent their own form. No recipe can replace this continual thought.'[27] For his own part, however, he can visualise only one direction for this intensive thought, a direction dictated by his belief that the Romantic exploration of the relationship between the human mind and nature represents a form of tyranny. Writing of the effect of film on the novel, he indicates the ideological significance of what he is doing as he contends that the actual presentation of objects, a chair, the movement of a hand, the bars to a window, reduces the amount of symbolism that can be associated with them: 'Instead of monopolizing our attention it seems just like one more attribute.' 'It seems in fact as if the conventions of photography . . . liberate us from our own conventions'. He goes on,

> . . . from now on . . . objects will gradually lose their instability and their secrets, they will forego their false mystery, and that suspect inner life that an essayist has called 'the romantic heart of things'. They will no longer be the vague reflection of the vague soul of the hero, the image of his torments, the shadow of his desires. Or rather, if it does still happen that things are used for a moment as a support for human passions, it will only be temporarily, and they will only be making a more or less derisive show of accepting the tyranny of meanings, the better to indicate how far they remain alien to man.[28]

In reading *A Passage to India* one is bound to be reminded of things that are said in that passage. Indeed, there are moments when Forster himself might seem almost to be ushering his readers towards a similar position. I am thinking in particular of Mrs Moore's journey to Bombay, and the scenes she sees from the train:

> She watched the indestructible life of man and his changing faces, and the houses he has built for himself and God, and they appeared to her not in terms of her own trouble but as things to see. There was, for instance, a place called Asirgarh which she passed at sunset and identified on a map – an enormous fortress among wooded hills. No one had ever mentioned Asirgarh to her, but it had huge and noble bastions and to the right of them was a mosque. She forgot it. Ten minutes later, Asirgarh reappeared. The mosque was to the left of the bastions now. The train in its descent through the Vindhyas had described a semicircle round Asirgarh. What could she connect it with except its own name? Nothing; she knew no one who lived there. But it had looked at her twice and seemed to say: 'I do not vanish.'   (xxiii, 213)

Once again, however, the position is not quite the same as in Robbe-Grillet's work. There the object is to be repeatedly observed and registered, unchanging, by the reader; at Asirgarh, by contrast, the object insists on its own stability, yet offers no point from which it can be viewed as a stable unit – it is either bastions and mosque or mosque and bastions: we understand the optical illusion that has disturbed Mrs Moore but are not permitted to focus on the object in its own identity. If we go on in spite of that to create our own stable image of Asirgarh, we are immediately brought up short by the next incidents. Mrs Moore too 'has started the machinery; it will work to its end' (xxii, 211). Just as the mechanical train, regarded as the point of her stability, made the identity of Asirgarh unnecessarily problematic to her, so her arrival at Bombay impresses her suddenly with a sense of what the machine is taking her away from:

> 'I have not seen the right places', she thought, as she saw embayed in the platforms of the Victoria terminus the end of the rails that had carried her over a continent and could never carry her back.   (xxiii, 214)

As she drives through Bombay she has a sudden longing to 'disentangle the hundred Indias that passed each other in its streets'. And then finally, as she boards the mechanical steamer that will take her back to England, she sees thousands of coconut palms waving her farewell.

'So you thought an echo was India; you took the Marabar Caves as final?' they laughed. 'What have we in common with them, or they with Asirgarh? Goodbye!'   (ibid.)

Forster has directed our attention to a particular object in space only to remind us immediately afterwards not only that there are myriads of objects to focus upon, but that the quality of our perception itself may change: that to hear an echo in a Marabar cave is not the same kind of experience as to respond to Asirgarh, and that even if we were to identify Asirgarh it would not be the same as to identify a myriad of coconut trees.

Forster's attitude to the stability of objects is, in that respect, diametrically opposed to Robbe-Grillet's. While recognising their ineluctable presence it would regard any attempt to give them finality as a form of enslavement. And he was sustained in this conviction by what he had learnt in pursuing the ways of the imagination. Like the early Romantics, he had come to know that the effort to hold together in the mind apparently irreconcilable modes of thought, called for by loyalty to different areas of one's psychic experience, could be, however oppressive in the short run, ultimately bracing and sustaining. The formula 'Each thing has a life of its own and we are all of one life'[29] had almost destroyed Coleridge by driving him to explore simultaneously the ultimate implications of objective and subjective states of mind, along with their moral implications, but it had also kept him faithful to the full range of human experience. Wordsworth's recognition in the Simplon Pass that the impossible contradictions of the landscape were yet held in unity by the imagination, that 'awful power' which could turn them into 'workings of one mind, the features / Of the same face, blossoms upon one tree', was equally liberating; the image of the journeying traveller could henceforth continue to alternate with that of the halted one. Blake's insistences on the supremacy of the imagination might lead him into grave impasses, but sustained him, equally, in his role as 'mental traveller'.[30]

This kind of dual consciousness is most fully sustained in *A Passage to India* by Professor Godbole, who continues to sing, even though the god neglects to come. His resilience and pursuant energy are demonstrated not only in the climactic dance scene (xxxiii, 283–4), where the contradictions of the world are almost (but not quite) brought into one, but also in his love of paradox – another trait shared with the Romantics. When asked his opinion about the alleged assault in the cave, for instance, he replies,

> 'My answer to that is this: that action was performed by Dr Aziz.' He stopped and sucked in his thin cheeks. 'It was performed by the guide.' He stopped again. 'It was performed by you.' Now he had an air of daring and coyness. 'It was performed by me.' He looked shyly down the sleeve of his own coat. 'And by my students. It was even performed by the lady herself. When evil occurs, it expresses the whole of the universe. Similarly when good occurs.'   (xix, 185–6)

In the same way Forster comments on the birth of Krishna,

> God is not born yet – that will occur at midnight – but He has also been born centuries ago, nor can He ever be born, because He is the Lord of the Universe, who transcends human processes. He is, was not, is not, was.   (xxxiii, 281)

I catch something of the same note in a recorded remark of Blake's. Talking to Crabb Robinson, he said firmly, 'Jesus is the only God' – and then he added, 'and so am I, and so are you'.[31]

Where Robbe-Grillet seeks to liberate his readers from the tyranny of imported meanings by directing them to see objects as ineluctably there, Forster seeks to liberate them by encouraging them to consider alternative meanings. His is ultimately a fiction of possibilities, of imaginative explorations which encourage his readers to be sceptical, yet also to be sceptical concerning their own scepticism. Perhaps there is something ultimately self-destructive about such a fictional enterprise, since consciousness of the multiplicity of meaning may lead rather to the fields of biography, criticism and social comment, – which Forster himself came to prefer. But it may also be that Forster, with his acute awareness of the possible play between imagination and object, ultimately was indicating a way forward for the novel to which the new novel, also, will prove to have been pointing. If so, the 'alertness to what has not yet been experienced' which provides the chief positive note in *A Passage to India* will come to have vindicated itself still more fully.

Conclusion: *A Passage to India* and the Versatility of the Novel

JOHN BEER

A Passage to India was more than ten years in the making, and Forster often despaired of completing it. Begun in 1913, shortly after he had visited India for the first time, it hung fire after the early chapters. The impact of the First World War and the experience of working in Alexandria changed his view of the world in important respects – after it, he said, he trusted people less and was quicker to impute cynicism – and it took him some time to catch up with such changes. When he returned to India in 1921 he took the pages of his unfinished manuscript with him, only to find that, as he said later, 'as soon as they were confronted with the country they purported to describe, they seemed to wilt and go dead. . . . The gap between India remembered and India experienced was too wide' (Introduction, p. 14; see above, p. 124). Finally, encouraged by Leonard Woolf, he completed it, but with a feeling of relief rather than triumph:

> I am so weary, not of working, but of not working: of thinking the book bad and so not working, and of not working and so thinking it bad: that vicious circle. Now it is done and I think it good.   (p. 19)

This might be compared with the more positive emotion of D. H. Lawrence, say, on completing *The Rainbow*: 'I have finished my *Rainbow*, bended it and set it firm. . . . I am *frightfully* excited over this novel now it is done.' Yet it is not altogether different from Lawrence's feelings on completing *Women in Love* (a novel closer to Forster's): 'The world of my novel is big and fearless – yes I love it, and love it passionately. It only seems to me horrible to have to publish it.' One recognises a similar alienation from potential readers – even if Lawrence is a good deal more assertive and combative in attitude.

In retrospect it is surprising that Forster should have been so tentative in recognising the quality of what is now generally agreed to be his most important novel, yet as we examine his achievement further we see that the tentativeness and the extent of his ambitions were linked in ways which may explain why such different interpretations of it have proved possible. The existence of such various approaches recalls the tale of the five blind men who went to visit an elephant, as related by G. K. Chesterton. The first seized its trunk and thought it to be a kind of serpent, another put his arm round its leg and believed it to be a tree; another leaned against it and found it a wall; another, taking hold of its tail, was convinced that it was a rope; while the last, running against its tusk, was equally convinced that it was a spear. Something of the same is true in the reading of a complex novel. The reader elects a particular approach (gained partly from previous fiction-reading) which aims to give a consistent interpretation, and proceeds to organise his or her reading around that approach. One will go to a novel for insight into its characters and skip impatiently over passages of description; another, interested in the historical background, may read those descriptions with great care while finding the characters less interesting; and so on. Meanwhile, it may be said, a good novel remains larger than any of the individual readers who pit themselves against it – larger even than the author himself, who may not fully have understood at the time what he was achieving. One of the reasons why we read other critics is to enlarge our vision of the work, to discover possible readings that differ from our own.

In the case of *A Passage to India* something further is involved. The comforting feature of the story of the blind men is that we know what an elephant is like: we find a secret pleasure in being able to reconcile the views of the blind men, whilst also finding our own sense of the elephant enhanced. In recent times, however, writers have been coming to terms with the fact that human beings might be like blind men living in a world where no one had ever seen an elephant at all. The European mind received many shocks in earlier centuries, many assaults on supposed certitudes; but it was always supposed that, if one probed deeply enough, a firm bedrock of fact would be found to exist, that rationality and kindliness must in some sense prevail and that human nature was fundamentally stable. In the early twentieth century, and particularly during and after the First World War, thinkers found themselves disturbingly visited by a sense (only occasionally prophesied in nineteenth-century thought) that there might be no stable order of things underlying experience, no ultimate truth on which human beings could rest.

Since then, this idea, strengthened by notions of relativity, has moved steadily into the foreground, to become a starting-point in literature as well as in thought. The particular achievement of Forster, however, was to have faced the recognition, yet also to have kept a firm hold on the idea that the various positive interpretations of the world could not after all be ignored, that the recognition of determinacy was, in one way, undermining to his art, since he had been brought up in a tradition which relied on characters remaining fundamentally the same. In his early novels he had excelled in showing human beings interacting with one another, sometimes revealing unexpected traits but giving no real reason to doubt their status as stable and self-conscious individuals. His inability to create characters in his Indian novel, by contrast, disturbed him even as he wrote it:

> Also there is a fundamental defect in the novel – the characters are not sufficiently interesting for the atmosphere. This tempts me to emphasise the atmosphere, and so to produce a meditation rather than a drama. (Introduction, p. 16)

Forster might seem here to be playing into the hands of those who have accused him of being a 'mystic'. What he did not say, however, and may not have recognised, was that the 'meditation' he was producing was not the kind of exercise which might have been recognised directly by a mystic; in its own making it was dramatic, rather, since it took into itself very diverse ways of looking at the world and allowed them to exist side by side. It could not aspire to the excitement or the passions which accompanied Lawrence's vision; Forster wished rather to stand back and allow views of the world which he found contending for supremacy in his mind to subsist together, interplaying in many different ways.

It should not, then, be assumed that one can read the essays in this volume and end by achieving a large, inclusive view of *A Passage to India*. What may rather be gained is a range of interpretations of human experience which enable one to detect different possible patterns of significance in the events. One learns, above all, that Forster's apparent lassitude and cynicism of tone (easily taken as the 'positive' element in the novel) may mask creativity which is very energetic.

That is one reason why the essays in this volume can take such diverse lines of approach. As both Wilfred Stone and John Drew point out here, and as Gillian Beer has demonstrated at greater length in chapter 4, it abounds in negatives; it begins by describing a city which presents 'nothing extraordinary' apart from some caves (which are in any case twenty miles away); it ends with an earth which says 'No, not yet' and a sky which says 'No, not there.' Yet as some of these critics also point out, one key to these negatives is to be found in Godbole's 'absence implies presence, absence is not non-existence'. To read and reread the novel, likewise, is to find oneself continually reversing or changing one's view of the events and their significance as different patterns of interpretation are suggested.

I   THE NOVEL AS DOCUMENTARY

The first thing that a reader coming to the novel might ask is, 'How true is this as a picture of India under British rule?' Dr Das's essay (Ch. 1) offers considerable help towards formulating an answer by documenting its events in terms of what was happening at the time when it was written. It is true of course that the novel can offer no more than a partial account of so vast a subject. The reader must bear in mind that its two main locations are based on places which were backwaters of British rule: Bankipore, the original of Chandrapore, was a small town in the north-east of India, Dewas a small Princely state where Forster himself served as secretary to a maharajah. The action of the novel is kept quite deliberately away from great centres such as Bombay, Calcutta and Delhi. A picture of British rule as a whole would have been bound to give attention to the higher ranges of the administration. The nearest Forster comes to such attention is in his brief, if pointed, account of the Lieutenant-Governor in chapter xxix.

Dr Das shows the accuracy of Forster's picture as an attempt to embody a possible state of affairs at that time. It is easy to argue that what happened in Chandrapore might not have happened in some other part of the country, or that other British officials might not have acted as these particular ones did; that, however, is ultimately to say (with Dr Aziz in the novel) that 'nothing comprehends the whole of India'. It should also be noted, as Dr Das himself acknowledges near the end of his essay, that Forster himself did not aim at total accuracy; he was content, for instance, to send scenes of which he was doubtful to one or two friends for comment and rely on their judgement. Some details also belong to the period of Forster's first visit in 1913 rather than to the period, ten years later, which provides a more obvious date for its events.

Dr Das ends by quoting Forster's comment that the novel must bear the marks of his own *accent*, so pointing to issues which are taken up by later essays in this collection; there are, however, some related issues which arise more directly from the questions under discussion in this essay. If a writer is writing a novel of any seriousness about a topic such as the British rule in India, it is likely to bear the marks of his own political philosophy.

Once we have formed our conclusions about the factual basis for the novel's events, therefore, we shall find ourselves turning to the attitudes of the writer himself as embodied in his interpretation of political relationships between societies and between the individual human beings that compose those societies. Forster's critique of British society in India owes a good deal to observations that he had made in his early fiction concerning middle-class society in England and in the English 'colonies' in European cities. At its worst he found it constrained by a narrow self-righteousness which inhibited individuals from looking at other nations with any curiosity or willingness to learn. (Not all the British in India were like this, of course: awareness among Indians of their own culture still owes much to European figures who became fascinated by it and devoted their lives to understanding it, but they were not generally to be found in places such as Bankipore.) Forster's own attitude was one of liberal–humanism: he believed that political action should be grounded in fundamental attitudes which respected freedom of action and the individuality of each human being. In the novel, however, he also comes to recognise the limits of such a political philosophy in depicting an indigenous society which would itself resist the adoption of such attitudes beyond a certain point. Forster's philosophy had grown up partly as a corrective to the constricted moral attitudes that were prevalent in certain sections of British society; it did not altogether explain, therefore, how one was to behave when dealing with areas of society where corruption was taken for granted.

These larger questions, involving as they do issues to which political philosophy is continually returning, have been the subject of several studies of Forster: F. C. Crews's *E. M. Forster: The Perils of Humanism*, for example [Booklist (f)], both recounts the development of his humanist attitude, and discusses its limitations. A searching account of his philosophy as it relates to the English experience of India has also been given by Benita Parry in her essay above (Ch. 3): she suggests that India at once evoked Forster's liberal humanism to the full and challenged it by the immensity of the problems presented. In the end, she argues, he saw his faith crumbling and could find no other.

A reading of the novel which is to pursue these further implications of Forster's critique will concentrate on two strains in it. First, it will see India as a testing-ground for the liberal–humanist attitude, with limited successes achieved by both Fielding and Mrs Moore, who might be described, respectively, as the 'liberal head' and 'liberal heart' of the novel; in this respect the novel offers some grounds for hope that human beings in every culture, whether Christian, Moslem or Hindu, will respond to an outgoing attitude of mind. Secondly, it will look at the limits which are drawn round such an approach: the accounts, for example, of the very real difficulties facing a magistrate trying to do justice; or of Mrs Moore's awakening to the forces which are alien to her hitherto unquestioned belief in the power of goodwill and kindness as guiding principles; or of the barriers encountered by Fielding in his endeavours to find an answer to India's problems through education. The clash between these elements gives depth to the novel as an attempt to interpret the social and political situation in British India.

The case may of course be put that with the decline of Western imperialism the issues presented in the novel have dated hopelessly. The idea of a Western power imposing its will on another large country – and claiming to do so in its own interests – is now less conceivable, even if the struggle to influence and even dominate such countries continues in less open ways. At that level the novel might be regarded simply as a historical document marking a stage in the evolution of anti-colonialism, its importance being primarily in its recounting of a state from which humanity has now emerged.

The more the interpretative elements in the novel are examined, however, the clearer it becomes that, even at the political level, the issues go well beyond the facts of imperialism as a historical phenomenon. They involve an encounter between Western political ideas and Eastern, and raise the question whether it is realistic to regard the liberal ideals which have come to the fore in Western culture as universal ideals which the whole world will eventually adopt in the course of a natural evolution. In addition, they look forward to the identification of more subtle forms of imperialism in cultural terms, as in the work of Edward Said and others. Many incidents in the novel bear on these questions, which remain relevant to the world situation so long as an interplay of Eastern and Western culture, each trying to assimilate and appropriate the other, persists.

II   THE NOVEL AS SYMBOLIC STATEMENT

Inasmuch as there are universal themes in the novel, they are likely to involve symbolism of some kind, as Wilfred Stone's essay (Ch. 2) indicates. Forster's statement that when he began the novel he knew that something important would happen in the caves but did not know what that event would be, seeing them primarily as an area where 'concentration' could take place, invites the reader to consider the Marabar expedition as particularly important from this point of view.

In one sense the caves are important simply by virtue of what they do to any human beings visiting them. In the same way an author might set at the centre of his novel a rock on which boats are wrecked, or a concentration camp, or a mountain of unusual difficulty: places where human capabilities are tested to their uttermost, where human relationships are put under strain, where the outlook of an individual may be altered for ever. The works of Conrad provide examples of this kind, as do the early novels of William Golding. It is not simply that the incident which takes place (or does not take place) in the caves (the alleged 'assault' on Adela Quested) provides the central event, or non-event, in the novel. The effects of the caves on the other characters – and notably upon Mrs Moore – are important for the liberal–humanist 'philosophy' of the novel, as discussed earlier, since they provide a dramatic illustration of the fact that nature herself is not necessarily on the side of a benevolent view of things but may show itself as indifferent, or even sinister.

At this point we begin to see that what the caves actually do to some individual characters, producing an effect of dull nightmare, cannot easily be separated from their wider significance. The physical effects of the echo on the human body, damping down all utterance and producing a stifling and crushing effect – particularly when encountered in a crowded atmosphere – are suggesting something important about nature at large.

At this level the cases are symbols, but of a very direct and obvious kind, since they participate in what they also represent. They are an essential part of the 'nature' which is being shown to be alien. It is not for nothing that the hills which contain them are seen as 'fists and fingers'. The caves are a part of the nature that is to be interpreted through them; and they present it in a form different from the popular version. Forster emphasises this point by his reference to Grasmere as he describes the visitors going up to the cave:

> 'Ah, dearest Grasmere!' Its little lakes and mountains were beloved by them all. Romantic yet manageable, it sprang from a kindlier planet. Here an untidy plain stretched to the knees of the Marabar.   (xiv, 150)

The growth of a sentimental view of nature had been a

marked feature of English culture in the eighteenth and nineteenth centuries, and for this reason Grasmere, written about with such affection by Wordsworth and others, and visited by many summer tourists before and after him, a peaceful vale where nature appeared at her most quiet and harmonious, was a natural point of focus for such feelings. (That Wordsworth himself was not a sentimentalist about nature is, of course, evident from *The Prelude* and some other works, where he shows his awareness that nature can show itself alien to human nature and its needs, but some of his more popular verses, taken by themselves, had encouraged less stringent attitudes.) During the twentieth century, a growing awareness of the other side to nature, already at work in the minds of writers such as Conrad and T. E. Hulme, was brought into focus by the events of the First World War. Forster, who had allowed the quiet English countryside to play an important part in his early works, and to provide a reconciliatory conclusion to *Howards End*, had himself been exposed to the bleaknesses first of India and then the Middle East; in this sense *A Passage to India* marks a new phase in his dealings with nature.

The echo in the cave has its own relationship to this question. As I have pointed out in an essay entitled 'Echoes, Reflections, Correspondences: Some Central Romantic Themes and *A Passage to India*', in *Approaches to E. M. Forster*, ed. V. A. Shahane (New Delhi, 1981), the tradition of the echo as a symbol of nature's benevolence goes back well before the Romantic movement in England. It is a favourite feature of Renaissance literature (where it takes up the figure of Echo from Greek mythology) and reappears from time to time throughout the history of English poetry. Often it acts as a reminder of the harmonies in nature – on a quiet summer's evening, for example. Even when it turns a speaker's final word or syllable back in ironic comment through the intervention of a different meaning, it still gives him the sense of living in a humanised world. Forster's echo in the cave takes the process into a new region by producing a dehumanised echo which neither reinforces a sense of harmony nor comments in human terms. It simply negates.

One cannot consider the role of the echo in the cave, however, without noticing the different part played by visual reflections. In the Marabar Caves the visual effects are as beautiful as those from the echoes are disturbing, with the result that the total experience cannot be regarded simply as sinister. Any discussion of the caves must take into account the polished walls and the beauty of the reflections there. How do they relate to the other, nightmarish effects?

So far we have thought of the caves as 'synecdochic' symbols: that is, as the kind of symbols where a part stands for a greater whole. Just as some nineteenth-century writers might have thought of Grasmere as a synecdochic symbol for nature when regarded a benevolent power, so the Marabar Caves may be regarded as the synecdochic symbol for her in her alien form. They are in continuity with all those other elements, deserts, snowy wastes, stormy seas, forest fires and bleak landscapes generally, which not only ignore human need but fail to project any image that might answer to the kindly elements in human nature.

As Wilfred Stone demonstrates, however, the caves are not simply synecdochic symbols, they are also symbolic images: they can be considered *in themselves* as images for certain kinds of human experience, independent of the nature in which they participate. To Mrs Moore, for instance, the nullity of the echo is an experience not simply of nature's indifference to her but of a more general alienation. She has always assumed that her own humanity will find an answering voice somewhere in the universe: she has never seriously doubted that the universe began with a voice saying, 'Let there be light', or that, when Christ in the moment of death said, 'It is finished', he was in some sense speaking with the voice of God as well as that of a human being. For the first time in her life it has come home to her that in the end there may be no answering voice in the universe. Her disorientation in the last stage of the novel is a baffled, muffled version of the complaint expressed eloquently by Rainer Maria Rilke at the opening of the *Duino Elegies*: 'Who, if I cried, would hear me among the angelic orders?'

Similarly, Adela Quested's reaction to the caves has less to do with nature than with her relationship to her fiancé and to Dr Aziz. During her conversation with him she has been at once forthcoming and withholding. On the one hand she has tried to express to him her hopes and fears for herself if she is to marry Ronny Heaslop and stay in India – her fears, for example, of becoming one of the typical Anglo-Indians she has encountered;

on the other she has failed to communicate with him on any topic which involves sexual attitudes: she is in a muddle concerning her own relationship with Ronny Heaslop which she cannot yet appreciate, and her incapability of understanding the complex attitudes of Dr Aziz is demonstrated when she gives him offence by asking whether he has more than one wife – even though in other respects he has a strongly sensual nature. 'Enter into the infinite labyrinth of another's brain / Ere thou measure the circle that he shall run', wrote William Blake: Adela's entry into the cave is symbolic of her entry into a relationship which she finds attractive but which is also baffling. It is the culmination of a thwarting which she had experienced previously in the novel, when she tried to talk directly to some of the Indians at the 'bridge party' but found that she 'strove in vain against the echoing walls of their civility'.

In such cases the caves are symbols of relationship for the individuals involved – actual to their outward perception yet also emblematic of their own human relationships, whether immediate or more general. From here it is a simple step to another grade at which the caves become psychic symbols, figuring forth the human unconscious itself. This use of the imagery goes back at least as far as the Romantics. We might think of Wordsworth's lines 'Caverns there were in my own mind / Which sun did never penetrate', or Shelley's 'inmost cave / Of man's deep spirit'. Modern critics, however, have found it more natural to read them primarily in terms either of Hindu religion or of Freudian psychology.

In the case of Hinduism, Glen O. Allen's essay 'Structure, Symbol, and Theme in E. M. Forster's *A Passage to India*' [Booklist (g)] may be consulted: it contains among other things the suggestion that the word 'ou-boum' which is used to describe the echo might bear some relationship (even if an ironic one) to the 'oм' of Hindu meditation. The Freudian imagery is discussed in Wilfred Stone's own book *The Cave and Mountain* [Booklist (b)]. Professor Stone further draws attention to a suggestion by Norman Douglas that the cave is an image of the womb in Hindu culture – though this suggestion should be treated with reserve in the absence of further supporting evidence.

Professor Stone's essay in the present collection sums up and extends these approaches to the caves by arguing that they might stand for the unconscious in all its rich human ambiguity. The Marabar Caves seem to be capable of generating vision as well as nightmare: they are described as 'eggs' as well as 'holes'. For Mrs Moore they are destructive, but, as she leaves India, we are told, thousands of palm trees wave farewell to her, saying 'So you thought an echo was final!' Inasmuch as the caves are symbolic they seem to be deeply ambiguous.

Study of the symbolism in the work can be further extended in two ways. First, the caves are not the only symbols there. As Reuben Brower pointed out in his essay 'The Twilight of the Double Vision', the titles of the novel's three sections, 'Mosque', 'Caves' and 'Temple', point to three important controlling images, each of which has to do with the relationships between British and Indians. Another important symbol is that of the bridge. Forster was fond of using it in his early work; a central image in *Howards End* is that of 'the rainbow bridge in us that should connect the prose and the passion'. When he first contemplated writing an Indian novel, he 'thought of it as a little bridge of sympathy between East and West', though later his growing sense of the gulf that needed to be spanned forbade anything so comfortable. That initial impetus seems to survive, however, in the satirical incident of the 'bridge party'; and the three main symbols of the novel (themselves set against a sky where it seemed that there must be 'something that over-arches all the skies . . . Beyond which again . . .') might be seen as those into which the original bridge image has collapsed. The mosque provides a definite, if limited, bridge between Mrs Moore and Dr Aziz; the expedition to the caves turns out to be no bridge at all, despite Aziz's hopes. And the temple with its festival? If that is a bridge it is a strangely inchoate one – the dominant imagery is of boats which go out of control, collide, and unite their passengers only as they fall into the water.

One line of investigation starting here might proceed into an inquiry whether there are other symbols in the novel, ramifying from these; another would take in other novels which imply large symbols, such as Dickens's *Bleak House* and *Little Dorrit*, Conrad's *Typhoon* and *Heart of Darkness*, D. H. Lawrence's *The Rainbow* and Virginia Woolf's *To the Lighthouse* and *The*

Waves. It can be argued that each of these writers uses symbolism in a different way, and much might be learned by comparing their varying methods.

III   THE LANGUAGE OF THE NOVEL

In trying to come to terms with this novel, we ought clearly to pay attention not only to its political thought and patterns of symbolism but to the language in which it is written. Before we notice the larger considerations and the extensive imagery noted above, we are likely to be struck by the very fine texture of the words; although Forster's technique of plot directs us to his larger effects, his excellence often lies in minute discriminations or subtle observations which may be forgotten if we direct ourselves too exclusively to larger patterns.

But how far can we be said to be actually hearing the author's voice? As Judith Herz points out (p. 155 below) Wilfred Stone has contended that in this novel editorial comment is almost entirely lacking – which is certainly true if one is comparing it with the author's earlier work, where he intervenes from time to time to explain what he thinks of the situation, or indicate his approval or disapproval of some comment by one of the characters; more recently, however, Barbara Rosecrance has taken issue with the view that he disappears totally from this novel, arguing by contrast that it is possible to demonstrate the 'dominating agency of Forster's narrative voice', a voice at once editorial and didactic (Herz, p. 156 below).

The opening pages of Professor Herz's contribution (Ch. 5) assist the discussion by showing how in this novel Forster is both author and ventriloquist. As he projects the flow of Ronny's speech in the opening pages the third-person narration means that we are listening to the reasonable, disinterested argument which is being put forward, yet also detect from such expressions as 'he did expect sympathy' an interested, personal tone in the voice that is delivering it – a double effect which Mrs Moore's own stream of consciousness is quick to distinguish. The most interesting sentence in the second paragraph quoted is, however, the last: 'One touch of regret . . . would have made him a different man, and the British Empire a different institution.' The conventions of reported thought in the novel are such that this might either be a further thought on Mrs Moore's part, or else be regarded as a detached reflection on the part of the narrator. And the somewhat orotund and generalised conclusion to the sentence makes it sound more like an authorial comment than a thought which would have come naturally to Mrs Moore, with her natural turn to the personal and sensitive. Forster thus achieves an interestingly poised effect, implying an endorsement of her thought without actually stating it. A somewhat similar effect may be observed in the well-known account of the effect of the echo on Mrs Moore after her experience in the cave ('If one had spoken vileness in that place or quoted lofty poetry, the comment would have been the same – "ou-boum" '). Since one cannot quite imagine Mrs Moore herself either speaking vileness or quoting lofty poetry in a Marabar cave, the idea is already projected away from her, and could be as readily a part of the narrator's own meditation. (As I have pointed out above (p. 107) moreover, it is relevant to observe that when Forster first drafted these incidents – see *The Manuscripts of 'A Passage to India'* [Booklist (a)] pp. 267–8 – they were assigned to Fielding, who actually quoted lofty poetry and received a dull echoing reply; it was only later that the idea was associated with Mrs Moore.) The effect of this distancing is to make one conscious of the author's voice at the expense of the characters and so to suggest an endorsement of the idea being expressed.

Attention to language repays the reader at every level. One should notice the extraordinary range of usages employed throughout, even in constructions and figures of speech. (A lecturer in English language has told me that he uses *A Passage to India* as a text book, not only for its contents but also because he finds he can illustrate from its pages almost every point that he wishes to make to his students about English usage.) Forster has a fine ear for delicate inflections of speech and what they may tell us about a speaker, or the culture from which that speaker comes. In the case of the English characters, a turn of phrase, or a piece of slang may signal a whole set of underlying assumptions.

What language are the Indians themselves to be thought of as speaking? During the process of revision, Forster considerably reduced the number of Indian words and also removed specific indications of what language was being spoken. Bikram K. Das assumes that within each linguistic community communication is total, thus implying that, the more idiomatic the English that the Indians speak, the more likely it is that they are speaking their own language ('A Stylistic Analysis of the Speech of the Indian Characters in Forster's *A Passage to India*' [Booklist (h)]). Santha Rama Rau makes a similar point: 'He persuades you . . . that the Indians are speaking to each other in their own language' – in *E. M. Forster: A Tribute*, ed. K. Natwar-Singh (New York, 1966) p. 57. If original intentions can be invoked, on the other hand, there is evidence that their primary language is English: 'They always spoke English together except in moments of excitement when they swirled into Urdu' (*The Manuscripts of 'A Passage to India'*, p. 7). Given some of Forster's major changes, particularly in connection with the episode in the cave, however, such an argument from first intentions must be treated with some reserve.

Kenneth Burke, in his book *Language as Symbolic Action* [Booklist (h)], has examined the novel's language from a different point of view, drawing attention to the way in which a word will be echoed here or there, setting up many patterns of possible association. A typical example:

> I had not watched '*star*', for instance. Yet, having been alerted, I noticed: A few lines after the opening of Chapter XXVII, when Fielding and Aziz are lying near each other in the night, at a time in the course of the plot when their friendship was closest, we are told:

> > Exactly above their heads hung the *constellation* of the Lion, the disc of Regulus so large and bright that it resembled a *tunnel*, and when this fancy was accepted all the other *stars* seemed *tunnels* too.

> The interesting thing here is that the *passageways* in the Caves are regularly called '*tunnels*'. In Chapter XVI, with regard to the *field glasses* that Miss Quested had dropped in her flight: 'They were lying at the verge of a cave, *half*-way down an entrance *tunnel*.' And from this passage one might radiate in another direction to the thought that the woman whom Fielding marries is named '*Stella*'. (p. 233)

The question of language can be pursued into the heart of the novel's achievement. A recent essay by Michael Orange, 'Language and Silence in *A Passage to India*' [Booklist (h)], examines the novel in terms of its 'sensitivity to its own verbal medium' (p. 143) and its progressively established 'distrust of verbalization'. Dr Orange points out that silence is usually important and worth attending to, since a moment of silence may indicate a point at which language has, for one reason or another, become impossible. This is true after Godbole has explained how his song inviting the Lord of the Universe to come to him is never answered. ('there was a moment of absolute silence. No ripple disturbed the water, no leaf stirred' – vii, 96) but it is also implicit in those incidents where characters simply respond to a ladder of difficult speculations by changing the subject to something trivial – as when the question whether beyond the sky there must not be something that overarches all the skies is sidestepped by a swift diversion into discussion of a current musical comedy (v, 60). These reiterated moments when language fails for one reason or another may suggest nihilism, but they also lend a note of mystery.

This aspect of the novel is investigated further by Gillian Beer in her essay 'Negation in *A Passage to India*' (Ch. 4). She points to the extraordinary pervasiveness of negative forms in the novel: not simply in the first and last sentences, as noted above, but on virtually every page. The role of the word 'nothing' (noted also by Wilfred Stone, p. 23 above) is seen by her to be crucial to an understanding of the novel as a whole, since it enacts ambiguity in an unusually intense manner. In one sense the word 'nothing' is likely to be the least noticeable word in a discourse, its negativity automatically excluding the reader's attention. But a word which is used so frequently becomes gradually more and more a presence; even more so once one's attention has been directed to it. It may also be seen to be relevant to the underlying cosmic questions. Just as Dr Orange shows that silence can make space for an experience of harmony, so absence may simply mark the space of a missing presence: in that case, Professor Godbole, with his 'absence implies presence' lives in a more realistic relationship to the universe than any of the other characters.

Many readers find it difficult to take Professor Godbole so seriously. He is often, after all, presented in a semi-comic light.

His prevarications in response to questions may also make him appear simply tiresome or foolish. There is a subtler reason, as well: much of what we learn about Godbole belongs to that side of the novel which has to do with description and local colour. There is a general tendency in the human mind to attend primarily to the dramatic elements in a novel – the action and the dialogue. Other effects are often thought to be largely ornamental in quality.

To such readers, the dominant tone of the language, in *A Passage to India*, picked up from the dialogue and the accounts of actions, is one of enlightened cynicism. The omnipresent negatives contribute to a weariness of tone; since Fielding is the character most directly central to action and dialogue, in fact, it is *his* tone which is likely to dominate in the reader's attention: admirably humane, dogged in perseverance towards the establishment of better relationships, yet also conscious of a strong likelihood of failure – at least in the short term.

Before accepting this reading of the novel too swiftly, however, one should give some attention to the 'musical' factors in the novel. Forster, as is well known, was extremely fond of music, particularly of Beethoven, and his earlier novels contain many references to it. His own study of fiction, *Aspects of the Novel*, includes a discussion of the quality he calls 'rhythm' (ch. viii). In his book *Rhythm in the Novel* [Booklist (h)], E. K. Brown discusses Forster at length from this point of view. For Brown, rhythm means primarily the recurrence of particular symbols, creating an atmosphere of expansion. He points to the wasps and bees and to the echo, as examples (pp. 93–103), and argues on a larger scale that the structure of the novel consists of 'three big blocks of sound', which have the 'rhythmic rise–fall–rise' that Forster himself found in *War and Peace* (p. 113). He also argues, from this point of view, that the novel is ultimately devoted not to Fielding's 'liberal, sceptical humanist values', but to 'values much better apprehended by Mrs Moore, who is irritable, of uncertain sympathies, in her time of crisis acridly intolerant, and who quotes only one author – St Paul'. He goes on, 'It should not be too much of a disturbance in interpreting a novel to find the author's imaginative sympathies outrunning his intellectual commitments', citing Turgenev as another artist to whom that happened (p. 114).

We shall return to this question concerning the 'centre' of the novel; for the moment it is enough to point out that the qustion of 'rhythm' can be pursued into its very texture. As Wilfred Stone points out towards the end of his contribution, some of these effects are very direct, as with the repetition of words or names three times over, or the chanting of 'Esmiss Esmoor'; a further reading on these lines would ask whether there are not subtler effects throughout the novel, working through the rhythms of the sentences and even of whole paragraphs. What effects are conveyed through the final sentences of the last chapter? Such an investigation is likely to proceed both narrowly, through minute examination of rhythmic effects, and broadly, through consideration of the role of music in general (including the part it may play in the organisation of patterns of symbols).

IV THE NOVEL AS IMAGINATIVE EXPRESSION

Investigation of the role of language brings out some very precise features of Forster's novel; it also, as we have seen, exposes some of its ambiguities. One learns among other things that much may depend on differing elements in the very language to which one is attending, so that conscious associations of the language may be counterpointed or even undermined by other effects which work largely in the subconscious.

John Drew's essay (Ch. 7) puts the issue fairly and squarely by arguing that the centre of the novel lies not with Fielding nor with Mrs Moore but with Professor Godbole. If we are looking for the unifying feature of the novelist, the element in him which holds all the others together, we shall find it, he argues, in Forster's covert self-identification with the vision by which Godbole lives. In support of this he is able to bring evidence of Forster's interest in Neo-Platonism during his time in Alexandria and to the resemblances between that philosophy (a philosophy which some claimed to be derived from India in the first place) and what is inherent in Godbole himself.

Some readers might resist such an interpretation, arguing that the 'meaning' of the novel must ultimately be determined by the amount of time devoted to other things, in comparison with the short spaces allotted to Godbole. On the other hand, attention to the imaginative and musical elements in the novel increases our awareness of the esoteric strains in the book. We may think, for example, of the peculiarly strong influence which Mrs Moore continues to exert after her departure and death, and of the indications of supernatural powers at work, or of the powerful role of ritual in the long festival scene. More important still is the experience which overtakes Adela Quested in the court room. In the eyes of the spectators she seems to suffer a bleak little collapse, resulting in the drear negative from her that upsets the course of the trial. But the reader, at least, is initiated into an awareness that inwardly her consciousness is not bleak; she is remembering the trip to the Marabar as a splendid occasion, full of lights and harmonies, and her realisation that she cannot locate Aziz in her memory as having followed her into the cave is in fact quite subsidiary to the larger imaginative vision that possesses her at that moment.

Elements such as these can be explained in various ways. Barbara Hardy, in *The Appropriate Form* [Booklist (i)], reads such things in terms of supernatural suggestion, whilst in *The Achievement of E. M. Forster* [Booklist (i)] I looked at them in the context of Forster's roots in Romanticism – not that more limited Victorian kind which too easily degenerated into nature sentimentalism, but the absolute kind associated with the early Romantics, which had to do with assertion of the power of imagination as a means of ultimate knowledge.

We do not necessarily need to choose between such interpretations. It might be argued that they simply exist side by side as potencies in the novel, inviting the reader to see its events from various vantage points.

Inasmuch as it is natural to try and reach a coherent interpretation, attention may be drawn to yet another pattern in the novel, pointed to by John Colmer in his essay 'Promise and Withdrawal in *A Passage to India*' in *E. M. Forster: A Human Exploration* [Booklist (e)]. He draws attention to the ways in which from an early age Forster showed an unusual sensitivity to experiences of disappointment, coupled with a capacity for further anticipation; and goes on to show how prominent a part such patterns of behaviour play in this novel – even to the rushing-together and parting again of the horses on the last page. The eager anticipation, followed by disappointment, in the Marabar expedition, is the culminating example of something that has appeared in several earlier chapters and is to recur. There is a constant sub-pattern of social encounters involving invitation, withdrawal, half-acceptance and rejection.

It is to this kind of interplay, a matter of continuing process rather than fixed scheme, that we might look for the most binding elements in the novel: it is the feature, certainly, which comes closest to including the cynical weariness at one extreme, and the underlying sense of music at the other.

It should not, however, be thought of as a 'final' quality. We cannot look for such finality without recalling the waving of the palm trees to Mrs Moore at the end of chapter xxiii: ' "So you thought an echo was India; you took the Marabar Caves as final?" they laughed. "What have we in common with them, or they with Asirgarh . . .?" ' The greatness of this novel lies not in a single vision communicated to the reader, but in the presentation of possibilities, strands to be followed, themes to be discovered. It is not the case that there is a final, harmonising reading which sums up all the others. As we concentrate on one strand, others may fall into the background, but they will retain their potency: the greatness of Forster's achievement corresponds with his success in allowing different strands to subsist together in the matrix of his creative mind.

We might for instance turn to the final sentences of the novel. Judith Herz offers one reading of them at the end of her piece, but acknowledges that others are possible. She points out, for example, that Alan Wilde, in 'Modernism and the Aesthetics of Crisis' [Booklist (h)], emphasises the formal elements of closure in the last sentence ('verbal repetitions, monosyllabic diction . . . formal parallelism, balance, alliteration . . .'), yet reads the final effect as a 'withdrawal of the artist from chaotic experience . . . into the containment of art' – acknowledging, at the same time, that 'the passage directs us thematically toward a distant, unresolved future' (p. 38). It seems to her, on the other hand, that thematically as well as syntactically one is left with both alternatives. In line with Wilde's reading, although using a very different mode of analysis, Molly Tinsley (Ch. 6) argues that the last sentence demonstrates Forster's failure finally to adapt the formal complex sentence to the formlessness of Indian experience (see p. 80 above).

What may be a failure in language, evidently, may equally be seen as a success from some other point of view. This is illustrated by the handling of the same incident in John Drew's essay (p. 89 above), where it is suggested that what still holds Aziz and Fielding together is the same India of many voices that spoke to Mrs Moore as she left it. Dr Drew also traces an important transition in the course of the novel from the theme of promise to that of appeal.

The multifacetedness of the last sentences is reflected in the novel as a whole: it is, among other things, a great novel of passiveness. To claim, with Kenneth Burke, that its point of view is 'designed to evoke in the reader a mood of ironically sympathetic contemplation' is perhaps to come as close as one can to an inclusive formula; but it is also to miss the point. For the sense of irony, the sympathy and the contemplative moods that are evoked refuse to remain yoked in a passive mode: they rise up in the reader's mind as active powers, causing further questionings, probings and cross-linkings. The essays we have looked at afford strong examples of such activity, but there are other modes, other readings (as the Booklist shows). In writing it, Forster showed what is possible when an artist lays himself open to the widest number of patterns of interpretation and leaves each to flourish, while exercising in addition the control that is requisite to the fashioning of a work that is expected (as he once pointed out in a moment of humorous deprecation) to 'tell a story'.

Notes

Place of publication is London unless otherwise stated. For abbreviations of Forster's works, see Key to References (also Booklist, which gives details of editions cited).

CHAPTER ONE. 'A PASSAGE TO INDIA': A SOCIO-HISTORICAL STUDY

1. *E. M. Forster: The Critical Heritage*, ed. Philip Gardner (1973).
2. In *Amrit Bazar Patrika*, 2 Feb 1922.
3. In *The Nation and Athenaeum*, 28 Jan 1922.
4. In *Blackwood's Magazine*, CCVII (Apr 1920) 441–6.
5. Nirad C. Chaudhuri, 'Passage to and from India', *Encounter*, II (June 1954) 19–24.
6. *Loc. cit.*, 442–6.
7. East India (Punjab Disturbances) 'Hunter Committee Report', presented to Parliament (1920), pp. 83–4.
8. Lord Hardinge, *My Indian Years: 1910–1916* (1948) pp. 86–7.
9. E. M. Forster, 'Indian Entries', *Encounter*, XVIII (Jan 1962) 26; repr. in *HD*, p. 223.
10. E. M. Forster, 'India and the Turk', *Nation and Athenaeum*, 30 Sep 1922, pp. 844–5.
11. Jawaharlal Nehru, *The History of the Indian National Congress*, ed. B. Pattabhai Sitaramayya (Bombay, 1946) p. 250.
12. See P. N. Furbank, *E. M. Forster: A Life* (1977–8) II, 125–30.

CHAPTER TWO. THE CAVES OF 'A PASSAGE TO INDIA'

1. E. M. Forster, 'The Art of Fiction', *Paris Review*, I (1953) 30–1.
2. See Wilfred Stone, *The Cave and the Mountain: A Study of E. M. Forster* (Stanford, Calif., 1966) p. 301.
3. E. M. Forster, 'The World Mountain', *Listener*, LI (1954) 978.
4. E. M. Forster, 'The Gods of India', *New Weekly*, 30 May 1914, p. 338.
5. *E. M. Forster: The Critical Heritage*, ed. Philip Gardner, p. 296.
6. Private interview with Woolf, Mar 1965.

7. C. J. Jung, *The Archetypes and the Collective Unconscious*, in *Collected Works*, IX.i (New York, 1959) 19–20.

8. One of the funniest uses of the term is by the missionaries Mr Sorley and old Mr Graysford trying to deal with the question of who or what shall be admitted into heaven. All races, to be sure, but the monkeys? jackals? wasps? oranges? cactuses? crystals? mud? bacteria? 'No, no, this is going too far. We must exclude someone from our gathering, or we shall be left with nothing' (iv, 58). But that idea of 'nothing' is no less meaningful for being in a comic context.

CHAPTER THREE. THE POLITICS OF REPRESENTATION IN 'A PASSAGE TO INDIA'

1. See Sara Suleri, 'Amorphous India: Questions of Geography', paper delivered at the Session on Colonial Discourse at the Meeting of the Modern Language Association of America, Dec 1983.

2. E. M. Forster, 'Art for Art's Sake' (1949), *Two Cheers for Democracy*, Abinger edn (1972) pp. 87–93.

3. E. M. Forster, 'Our Diversions: 2, The Birth of an Empire' (1924), in *AH*, pp. 44–7; 'The Challenge of our Time' (1946), in *Two Cheers*, pp. 54–8.

4. Rape in British–Indian writing, both during and after the Raj, invariably represents the assailant, putative or proven, as Indian and the victim as British, an allocation of roles which inverts the historical situation. It would seem that the 'India' constructed by the Raj discourse, and egregiously apparent in Anglo-Indian romances, became a figure of sexual menace threatening to violate British values.

5. A call echoed in Forster's need for a perfect Friend.

6. Walt Whitman, 'Passage to India' (1871) in *Leaves of Grass* (New York, 1965); Edward Carpenter, 'India, the Wisdom-Land' (1890) in *Toward Democracy* (1911). In his essay 'Edward Carpenter' (1944), Forster wrote, 'As he had looked outside his own class for companionship, so he was obliged to look outside his own race for wisdom' (*Two Cheers*, p. 207). It is open to conjecture that the predominantly 'feminine' nature of India's civilisations, their cultivation of the imagination and intuitions, the pursuit of the unseen, and an eroticism in the visual arts, myths and epics which is conceptually androgynous – the Absolute as the two-in-one, the male–female principles as coexistent – may have had an especial appeal to male members of what Carpenter called the intermediate sex.

7. Quoted in Furbank, *E. M. Forster*, I, 216.

8. Heinrich Zimmer, *Philosophies of India* (1967) p. 231 (first published 1952).

9. The significance of Jain cosmology to the ideas and images in 'Caves' is discussed in my *Delusions and Discoveries: Studies on India in the British Imagination 1880–1930* (1972).

10. E. M. Forster, 'Liberty in England' (1935), in *AH*, pp. 62–3.

11. In addition to the works referred to in these notes I wish to acknowledge a more general debt to the following books: John Beer, *The Achievement of E. M. Forster* (1962); *E. M. Forster: 'A Passage to India'. A Selection of Critical Essays*, ed. Malcolm Bradbury, Casebook series (1970); Frederick C. Crews, *E. M. Forster: The Perils of Humanism* (1962); June Perry Levine, *Creation and Criticism: A Passage to India* (1971); Edward Said, *Orientalism* (1978); Stone, *The Cave and the Mountain*; Lionel Trilling, *E. M. Forster* (1944); Peter Widdowson, *E. M. Forster's 'Howards End': Fiction as History*, Text and Context series (1977).

CHAPTER FOUR. NEGATION IN 'A PASSAGE TO INDIA'

1. Pierre Macherey, *Pour une théorie de la production littéraire* (Paris, 1974) p. 258.

2. For discussion of the syntactic functions of negation see, for example, Edward Klima, 'Negation in English', in *The Structure of Language*, ed. J. A. Fodor and J. J. Katz (1964); John Lyons, *Semantics* (Cambridge, 1977) II, 768–77; and the work of Ray Cattell.

CHAPTER FIVE. LISTENING TO LANGUAGE

1. Two essays which deal with this question have other concerns as their primary emphases: social comedy in Kenneth Burke, 'Social and Cosmic Mystery: *A Passage to India*', *Language as Symbolic Action* (Berkeley, Calif., 1966) pp. 223–39; and symbolic metaphor in Reuben Brower, *The Fields of Light* (New York, 1951; 1962). See also, for other fiction, David Lodge, *Language of Fiction: Essays in Criticism and Verbal Analysis of the English Novel* (1966); Gillian Beer, '*One of Our Conquerors*: Language and Music', in *Meredith Now: Some Critical Essays*, ed. Ian Fletcher (1971) pp. 265–80; Norman Page, *The Language of Jane Austen* (Oxford, 1972) and *Speech in the English Novel*, English Language series (1973).

2. There has been little agreement about the degree of authorial presence in the novel. Stone, for example, argues that editorial comment 'is almost entirely lacking' (*The Cave and the Mountain*, p. 340); Barbara Rosecrance takes issue with this and demonstrates

'the dominating agency of Forster's narrative voice', a voice that she describes as both editorial and didactic – *Forster's Narrative Voice* (Ithaca, NY, 1982) pp. 184–237. Gerard Genette's distinction between voice and vision and his chapters on narrative levels and moods are particularly illuminating for establishing discriminations between the controlling voices in Forster's text: *Narrative Discourse: An Essay in Method* (Ithaca, NY, 1980).

3. Walt Whitman, 'Passage to India', *Leaves of Grass*, ll. 121–3.

4. There is an interesting anticipation here of Adela's intuition, after the catastrophe, that 'in space things touch, in time things part'. Burke, in *Language as Symbolic Action*, p. 235, points out how this 'vatic remark . . . ambiguously foretells the end of the novel'.

5. See Elizabeth Barrett, 'Comedy, Courtesy and *A Passage to India*', *English Studies in Canada*, x (1984) 77–93, for a discussion of this scene in terms of its movements of withdrawal and invitation.

6. V. J. Emmett, Jr, 'Verbal Truth and Truth of Mood in E. M. Forster's *A Passage to India*', *English Literature in Transition*, xv (1972) 199–212, uses the distinction that Forster has Fielding make, to provide a reading of the novel where the Indian characters generally observe the latter, the British the former kind of truth.

7. 'Language comes to stand for everything that divides men; while memory and silence stand for what reconciles and unites' – John Colmer, *E. M. Forster: The Personal Voice* (1975) p. 168. Colmer is, however, exceptionally sympathetic to the nuances of voice. He sees the 'superiority' of the novel resting 'as much on the triumph of voice as the triumph of vision' (p. 172).

8. Michael Orange reads this moment quite differently: 'With the departure of the intrusive Heaslop the meaning of song infuses the entire scene . . . the words do not approach enactment but figure as sign-posts to a condition of feeling that is the antithesis of ratiocination and therefore of language.' – 'Language and Silence in *A Passage to India*', in *E. M. Forster: A Human Exploration*, ed. G. K. Das and J. B. Beer (1979) p. 157. The implication is that that is the direction in which the novel is moving.

9. *The Manuscripts of 'A Passage to India'*, ed. Oliver Stallybrass (1978) p. 144.

10. The degree to which Forster follows out the implications of his own metaphors and discovers his meaning through the language he uses is explored in P. N. Furbank, 'Forster and "Bloomsbury" Prose', in *E. M. Forster: A Human Exploration*.

11. F. R. Leavis, 'E. M. Forster' (1938), in *The Common Pursuit* (1952) p. 294.

CHAPTER SIX. MUDDLE ET CETERA: SYNTAX IN 'A PASSAGE TO INDIA'

1. G. W. Turner, *Stylistics* (Harmondsworth, Middx: Penguin, 1973) p. 71.

CHAPTER SEVEN. THE SPIRIT BEHIND THE FRIEZE?

1. Strabo *Geographia*, xv.i.59, 63–5.
2. For instance, Porphyry, 'Life of Plotinus', ch. iii, and 'On Abstinence', iv.17–18; Apuleius, 'Florida', xv, in *Works*, trs. unnamed (1853); and Apollonius in *In Honour of Apollonius of Tyana*, trs. and ed. J. S. Phillimore, 2 vols (Oxford, 1912). Incidentally, Forster stayed with Phillimore in 1907.
3. Robert de Nobili in *Purchas his Pilgrimage*, 4th edn (1626) v, 558–9; G. P. Marana, W. Bradshaw, *et al.*, *The Eight Volumes of Letters Written by a Turkish Spy* (1694); J. Z. Holwell, *A Review of the Original Principles, Religious and Moral, of the Ancient Brahmins* (1779); Thomas Maurice, *Indian Antiquities* (?1793–1800); Sir William Jones, *Works*, ed. Lord Teignmouth (1807). The first translation from the Sanskrit, *The Bhagvat-Geeta*, trs. Sir Charles Wilkins (1785) was reviewed in terms of Platonism. An important modern comparison is made by J. F. Staal in *Advaita and Neoplatonism* (Madras, 1961).
4. E. M. Forster, *Alexandria: A History and a Guide* (Alexandria, 1922) pp. 65–8. See also Forster's review 'The Gods of India' (1914), in *Albergo Empedocle and Other Writings by E. M. Forster*, ed. George H. Thomson (New York, 1971) p. 222. Forster, like the reviewers of Wilkins' translation, may have recognised parallels in the *Gita* (see his 1912 essay, 'Hymn before Action', in *AH*, pp. 332–4).
5. *Plotinus: The Ethical Treatises* [etc.], trs. and ed. Stephen MacKenna, 5 vols (London, 1917–30), vol I of which is acknowledged in *Alexandria*. Vol I substantially covers the whole of the *Enneads*. The basic shape of the Neo-Platonist argument is discernible even in Ennead I, which is composed of tractates on the Animate and the Man; the Virtues; Dialectic (the Upward Way); True Happiness (including a portrait of the ideal sage); Happiness and Time; Beauty (from which Forster quotes directly); the Primal Good and Secondary Forms of Good; and on the Nature and Source of Evil. Quite apart from this and a 'Note on Terminology' (upon which Forster again draws directly) there is a 'Conspectus of the Plotinian System' which offers extracts from all six Enneads, primarily on the Soul and on the Supreme. Lowes Dickinson, with whom Forster first went to India and whose biography he wrote, was, previously to MacKenna, the only lucid English commentator on Plotinus (unpublished Fellowship dissertation, King's College, Cambridge).
6. See also *Enneads*, v.v.8–9; vi.iv.2, ix.7, 14. Coleridge, possibly

with Plotinus in mind, touches on the debilitating experience of 'God present without manifestation of his presence' in *Biographia Literaria*, ed. J. Shawcross (Oxford, 1907) ii.xxiv (p. 208).

7. Gokal, the Brahmin in L. H. Myers, *The Root and the Flower* (1935), quotes Plotinus to summarise his philosophy (pp. 186, 217).

8. Cf. *Enneads*, vi.ix.9; Heinrich Zimmer, *Myths and Symbols in Indian Art and Civilization*, ed. Joseph Campbell (New York, 1962) p. 26.

9. Coleridge uses this passage centrally in *Biographia Literaria*, i, xii (pp. 166–7).

10. Fielding experiences the possibility of idealism (*PI*, xxvi, 249).

11. In Forster's 1921 essay on Babur (*AH*, pp. 292–6), the Mogul love of detail is set over against the ways of a Hindu race 'which has never found moral or aesthetic excellence by focussing upon details'.

12. See also *PI*, ii, 37, 40–2; xi, 133. The Moslem love of poetry is again emphasised in ix, 118–19; xxxi, 273. However, it is the poetry of nostalgia ('Gone, gone' – xxx, 266) and not of appeal ('Come, come').

13. Fielding had earlier noted the emotional use of language (vii, 88; xi, 129). The Marabar expedition itself would not have taken place had not Aziz found his words being taken literally (vii, 86–7, 91). See also ii, 35, 45; iv, 57; vi, 74, 76–7; vii, 81, 84; viii, 108; ix, 125; xi, 128; xiv, 157; xv, 162, 163, 168.

14. Cf. *Enneads*, i.iv.7. Godbole concurs with Plotinus on the subject of patriotism (*PI*, xxxiv, 290).

15. 'The Ballad of the East and West', first and last stanzas, in *A Choice of Kipling's Verse*, ed. T. S. Eliot (1963) pp. 111–16.

16. The hundred mouths of India all echo Godbole's 'Come, come' (*PI*, xiv, 149). Mrs Moore longs to disentangle the hundred Indias (xxiii, 214). Fielding is incapable of judging whether the hundred Indias are one (xxix, 261).

17. This view is consonant with the 'neti, neti' philosophy of the oldest Upanishads: e.g. *Brihad Aranyaka*, ii.iii.6, iii.ix.26; iv.ii.4, in *The Thirteen Principal Upanishads*, trs. R. E. Hume, 2nd rev. edn (1931) pp. 39–40, 97, 125, 132.

18. Staal, *Advaita and Neoplatonism*, p. 224.

19. Ibid., pp. 133–42.

20. See Zimmer, *Myths and Symbols*, pp. 35–45, 193–4.

21. At first Mrs Moore, like Adela later, believes she has been attacked by a *person*. The caves are a challenge not to morality ('good or evil' – *PI*, xii, 139) but to the Imagination.

22. For the importance of 'sounds' see the next paragraph of this article. Adela eventually speaks of being indebted to India (xxxvi, 303).

23. 'She is not here, and consequently she can say nothing' (xxiv, 229).

24. Forster's Hindu Brahm is here identical with 'That Other' sought by 'the lesser gods' of Plotinus (*Enneads*, vi.v.12).

25. The 'Temple' section of *A Passage to India* opens (as well as closes) with references to the limitations of time and place which Hindu devotions seek to transcend. The mystical state gives meaning to the phrase which haunted Adela in her delirium: 'In space things touch, in time things part' (xxii, 199). According to Plotinus time is the life of the Soul in movement as it passes towards enlightenment, and the Soul is the space within which the whole visible Cosmos moves. As the Soul returns to rest, time is reabsorbed into eternity and the Cosmos realises its ideal (*Enneads*, iii.vii.6, 11–12).

26. For one moment only Aziz experiences a similar disillusionment with personal relationships (*PI*, xxx, 267).

27. The sound of Mrs Moore's name causes him to believe she is 'coming to help him' (xxxv, 298).

28. Ronny misses the significance altogether. He is quite right to suppose there is something subversive about the *mali* outside his window picking up 'sounds' (xxii, 207), just as he is about there being 'a connecting thread' which undermines British rule (xxxvi, 303). But he is wholly unaware that the implications are as cosmic here as they are when his peon, Krishna, in his mundane way, imitates the god his namesake by neglecting to come at call (viii, 111).

29. This limiting, because dualistic, definition plunges Aziz into the cycle of 'mosque, caves'. Cf. a similar antithesis established by Coleridge, cited in John Beer, *Coleridge the Visionary* (1959) p. 247.

30. Forster is being ironic when he alludes to those who refer to 'the toiling ryot' as 'the real India' (*PI*, xxxiii, 281) only in so far as he is aware that here, as elsewhere, he has concurred with an Anglo-Indian attitude (xiv, 148–9).

31. 'Passage to India', section ix, ll. 233–4, in *Walt Whitman: The Complete Poems*, ed. Francis Murphy (Harmondsworth, Middx, 1975) p. 436.

32. The water-chestnut gatherer, separated from Godbole by an enormous social gulf, is one with him in the appeal to God; the punkah wallah confronts Mr Das with the proposition that a man can not only control a court according to British legal procedures but be the god whose breath alone gives life to the world of dust; the servitor, who is as immobile in the cosmic storm on the lake as the punkah wallah was during the racial storm in the court room, has a hereditary power even greater than that evident at Udaipur, where the coronation of the ruler is made dependent on anointment by a servant. The other Hindus, like Krishna the peon, echo cosmic truths (the Bhattacharyas, for example, about the relationship of absence and presence; the villagers near the Marabars, about the relationship of illusion and reality).

33. Cf. terminology used in *Enneads*, iv.iv.6; vi.iii.3.

34. Cf. *Enneads*, vi.vii.22. Plotinus also associates beauty and radiance with Vision in v.viii.10; vi.vi.18, vii.21, 36. For ref. to Vision 'indwelling' and the reversion to 'individual clods', cf. Porphyry, 'Life of Plotinus', ch. x; *Enneads*, iii.viii.6 and vi.ii.21.

35. For Forster and Plotinus on the life of stones, cf. *PI*, xv, 161; *Enneads*, iv.iv.27; and of mountains, cf. *PI*, xii, 137; *Enneads*, vi.vii.11.

36. The festival has been 'a frustration of reason and form' (*PI*, xxxiii, 282). The 'Temple' section Forster referred to as 'a lump' – *Writers at Work*, ed. Malcolm Cowley (1958) ser. 1, p. 27. He has followed Plotinus in taking Hellenism beyond its traditional commitment to reason and form.

37. *AN*, vii, 92 (in the light of initial remarks on pp. 2, 4, 30). In this climactic chapter vii, the hallmark of good fiction is said to be something quite alien to common sense – its bardic quality, its tone or sound, which Forster likes to describe as 'song' (pp. 86, 93, 94, 99). See also viii, 116.

38. E. M. Forster, 'Anonymity: An Inquiry', in *Two Cheers*, pp. 95–6. The last sentence here is almost certainly a Coleridgean echo, since Coleridge is named as a point of reference throughout the essay. For this final, unreserved commitment to the Imagination, Forster quotes Shelley directly (p. 101). In 'Notes on the English Character' (1920), the one Englishman named by Forster as having, in the context of (the original of) the Aziz–Fielding argument on emotion (*PI*, xxxvii, 253), an Oriental belief in the endlessness of the spirit is Shelley (*AH*, p. 6).

39. Strictly speaking, in Neo-Platonist terms (and thus those of this reading of the novel), it is wrong to speak of spirit being embodied – a body exists in spirit and not spirit in body (*Enneads*, iv.iii.20). Forster appreciates this distinction in *AN*, vii, 91–2.

40. Incidentally, Godbole is a poet – but one who has to be 'divined' since we never hear his poems (*PI*, xxxi, 265).

41. Most recently by Edward Said, in *Orientalism* (1978). Aziz recognises that even 'seeing India' is a form of ruling it (*PI*, xxxvi, 301).

42. See n.1. The Alexander romances in particular led medieval Europe to identify the East with India, even on its maps – see George Cary, *The Medieval Alexander*, ed. D. J. A. Ross (Cambridge, 1956); Kirtland Wright, *The Geographical Lore of the Time of the Crusades* (New York, 1925). In spite of the discovery of China and the Farther East, this identification often prevailed in minds shaped by a classical education, especially in the closing decades of the eighteenth century when the British established an empire in India.

43. Cary, *The Medieval Alexander*, *passim*.

44. Conversely, the rational, sceptical ethos of the British, for

whom information is great and shall prevail (*PI*, xx, 197), is shown, even at its best, to be not only inadequate but also ineffective.

45. Made evident in Jones's series of discourses on the peoples of Asia in the first three vols of *Asiatic Researches* (Calcutta, 1788–92).

46. Two Upanishads postulating this which especially attracted Yeats were the *Brihad Aranyaka* and the *Mandukya* Upanishads (Hume, pp. 98–147, 391–3). For the relationship of formed to formless Brahma, see p. 97.

47. 'Kubla Khan'. The orientalism of the 1790s was centred on Jones's researches in India. See also 'Kublai Khan: the Rise of Tantric Buddhism', *Adam*, XLI, 416–18 (1979) 73–80.

48. Shelley, *Prometheus Unbound*. This work, which happens to be consonant with Kashmiri mythology, is shaped by two 'Indian' works inspired by Jones's researches: Robert Southey, *The Curse of Kehama* (1810); Sydney Owenson, *The Missionary*, 3 vols (1811).

49. To take an example from another 'Oriental' tradition, Jerusalem is never so firmly built in England's green and pleasant land as in a running line of Blake's verse.

CHAPTER EIGHT. 'A PASSAGE TO INDIA', THE FRENCH NEW NOVEL AND ENGLISH ROMANTICISM

1. Beer, *The Achievement of E. M. Forster*, ch. 6.

2. John Beer, 'Echoes, Recollections, Correspondences: Some Central Romantic Themes and *A Passage to India*', in *Approaches to E. M. Forster*, ed. V. A. Shahane (New Delhi, 1981), papers presented at the Forster centenary conference in Hyderabad, India, Jan 1979.

3. See esp. Frank Kermode, *The Classic* (1975).

4. Alain Robbe-Grillet, *Snapshots, and Towards a New Novel*, trs. B. Wright (1965) p. 56.

5. Ibid., pp. 83–4.

6. E. M. Forster, *The Manuscripts of 'A Passage to India'*, ed. Oliver Stallybrass, (1978) pp. 267–8.

7. John Sturrock, *The French New Novel: Claude Simon, Michel Butor, Alain Robbe-Grillet* (1969) pp. 178–9, 187–8.

8. Robbe-Grillet, ibid., p. 194.

9. See, for example, Burgundy in 'The French Revolution', ll. 83–105, and Urizen in *The Four Zoas*, ii.135–200, in *Complete Writings of William Blake*, ed. Geoffrey Keynes (1957) pp. 138–9, 282–5. Cf. my *Blake's Humanism* (Manchester, 1968) pp. 98–102, and *Blake's Visionary Universe* (Manchester, 1969) pp. 139–47, etc.

10. 'There is No Natural Religion', in *Complete Writings of Blake*, p. 97.

11. Sturrock, quoting *Le Voyeur* (Paris, 1955), *The French New Novel*, p. 216.

12. Letter to G. Lowes Dickinson, 26 June 1924, quoted in the Introduction to *PI*, p. 26.

13. Forster, *The Manuscripts of 'A Passage to India'*, p. 499.

14. See G. O. Allen, 'Structure, Symbol and Theme in E. M. Forster's *A Passage to India*', *PMLA*, LXX (1955) 942–3; and Stone, *The Cave and the Mountain*, p. 310.

15. See Forster's pieces in the *Listener*, 2 Dec 1954, pp. 977–8; and 5 Dec 1940, pp. 801–2.

16. Stone, *The Cave and the Mountain*, p. 301.

17. *Writers at Work: The Paris Review Interviews*, ed. Malcolm Cowley (1958) pp. 26–7.

18. Leavis, *The Common Pursuit*, p. 274. What Leavis sees as a failing at this point may more profitably be viewed as a complex effect. See my discussion in *The Achievement of E. M. Forster*, pp. 190–2, and Judith Herz's above, p. 69.

19. P. N. Furbank, 'The Personality of E. M. Forster', *Encounter*, xxxv (Nov 1970) 67.

20. Review of Lawrence Binyon, *Poems of Blake*, *Spectator*, 2 Apr 1932, p. 274.

21. See 'The Human Abstract', William Blake, *Songs of Innocence and Experience*, facsimile with an introduction and commentary by Geoffrey Keynes (New York, 1967) plate 47; and my discussion in *Interpreting Blake*, ed. M. Phillips (Cambridge, 1978) pp. 215–16. Forster's own copy of the illuminated *Songs*, one of the most beautiful executed by Blake, is now in the library of King's College, Cambridge.

22. Robbe-Grillet, *Snapshots*, p. 156.

23. See Keats's annotation to *Paradise Lost* in *The Poetical Works and Other Writings of John Keats*, ed. Harry Buxton Forman (1883) III, 24.

24. E. M. Forster, 'The Art and Architecture of India', *Listener*, 10 Sep 1953, p. 420.

25. Rabindranath Tagore, *Gitanjali* (1913) pp. 36–7. There is, of course, a strong yearning and waiting effect in Tagore's poem also (see, for example, pp. 32–4).

26. Robbe-Grillet, *Snapshots*, pp. 54–5.

27. Ibid., pp. 42, 47.

28. Ibid., pp. 54–5.

29. See Clement Carlyon, *Early Years and Late Reflections* (1856) I, 193; and cf. *Collected Letters of Samuel Taylor Coleridge*, ed. Earl Leslie Griggs (Oxford, 1956) II, 866: 'In the Hebrew Poets each Thing has a Life of its own, and yet they are all one Life'.

30. Wordsworth, *The Prelude* (1850) VI, 592–640; *Complete Writings of William Blake*, pp. 424–7; and see my *Wordsworth and the*

Human Heart (1978) esp. pp. 240, 252–3, and *Wordsworth in Time* (1979) pp. 158–61.

    31. *Henry Crabb Robinson on Books and their Writers*, ed. E. J. Morley (1938) i, 326.

Booklist: Texts and Further Reading

(a) TEXTS

All quotations from *A Passage to India* (*PI*) are taken from the Penguin reprint of the Abinger edition, ed. Oliver Stallybrass (Harmondsworth, Middx, 1979). See p. x above for key. The hardback edition of this volume was accompanied by another, *The Manuscripts of 'A Passage to India'* (1979), which is important to anyone studying its growth. The introductions to these two volumes give an excellent account of many matters connected with the novel. Quotations from Forster's other works are from the hardback Abinger edition, where at present available, otherwise from the first editions (chapter numbers are given, where appropriate, to assist readers working from other editions). *Howards End* is quoted from the Abinger edition, ed. Oliver Stallybrass (1978); for other works by Forster cited, see following.

(b) RELATED WRITINGS BY FORSTER

For background material in Forster's own writings, his book *The Hill of Devi* (1933) should be consulted, along with essays such as 'The World Mountain', *Listener*, LI (1954) 978; 'The Gods of India', *New Weekly*, 30 May 1914; and the essays in Part IV of *Abinger Harvest* (1936: *AH*). Further Indian writings are included in the 1983 Abinger edition of *The Hill of Devi* (*HD*).

Forster's views concerning the novel as a literary form are set out in *Aspects of the Novel* (1927; Abinger edn 1974: *AN*). The essay 'Anonymity: An Inquiry', in *Two Cheers for Democracy* (1957; Abinger edn 1972), and the interview reproduced in the *Paris Review*, I (1953), repr. in *Writers at Work*, ed. Malcolm Cowley (1958) also contain valuable observations on his part.

The reception of *A Passage to India* may be traced through Philip Gardner's collection of contemporary reviews and comments in *E. M.*

Forster: The Critical Heritage (1973). The best long study of Forster's work in general is Wilfred Stone's *The Cave and the Mountain* (Stanford, Calif., 1966); the standard biography is by P. N. Furbank: *E. M. Forster: A Life*, 2 vols (1977–8). The *Selected Letters* (1983–5) also contain many references to India.

(c) BIBLIOGRAPHIES

For good brief critical bibliographies of Forster, see Malcolm Bradbury's section in *The English Novel: Select Bibliographical Guides*, ed. A. E. Dyson (Oxford, 1958) and F. P. W. McDowell's in *E. M. Forster: A Human Exploration* and *E. M. Forster: Centenary Revaluations* [section (e) below]. An exhaustive bibliography of secondary works is to be found in McDowell's *E. M. Forster: An Annotated Bibliography of Secondary Writings on Him* (Northern Illinois University Press, 1977).

(d) STUDIES OF 'A PASSAGE TO INDIA'

Many critics have written well on *A Passage to India*. Apart from the studies represented in the present volume, interesting and varying lights on the novel can be gained by reading a range of articles such as F. R. Leavis, 'E. M. Forster', 1938 essay in *Scrutiny*, repr. in *The Common Pursuit* (1952); Reuben Brower, 'The Twilight of Double Vision: Symbol and Irony in *A Passage to India*', in *The Fields of Light* (New York, 1951); Hugh Maclean, 'The Structure of *A Passage to India*', *University of Toronto Quarterly*, XXII (1953) 157–71; John Dixon Hunt, 'Muddle and Mystery in *A Passage to India*', *ELH*, XXXIII (Dec 1966); and Malcolm Bradbury, 'Two Passages to India: Forster as Victorian and Modern', in *Aspects of E. M. Forster* [section (e) below]. A good introduction to the novel will be found in John Colmer's small volume in the Studies in English Literature series (1967). In addition, many books on Forster will be found to have an illuminating chapter on this novel, to be read in the light of the author's larger discussion.

(e) COLLECTIONS OF STUDIES

Some of the best previous studies of this novel have been collected by Malcolm Bradbury in *E. M. Forster: 'A Passage to India'. A Selection of Critical Essays*, Casebook series (1970) and by Andrew Rutherford in *Twentieth Century Interpretations of 'A Passage to India'* (Englewood Cliffs, NJ, 1970).

Recent collections of original studies of Forster's work include *Aspects of E. M. Forster*, ed. Oliver Stallybrass (1969); *E. M. Forster: A Human Exploration* ed. G. K. Das and J. B. Beer (1979); *E. M. Forster: Centenary Revaluations*, ed. J. S. Herz and R. K. Martin (1981).

(f) SOCIAL AND POLITICAL ASPECTS (CHS 1, 3)

Lionel Trilling, *E. M. Forster: A Study* (1944).

Nirad C. Chaudhuri, 'Passage to and from India', *Encounter*, II (June 1954), 19–24.

F. C. Crews, *E. M. Forster: The Perils of Humanism* (Princeton, NJ, 1962).

G. K. Das, *E. M. Forster's India* (1977).

Robin Jared Lewis, *E. M. Forster's Passages to India* (New York, 1979).

Benita Parry, *Delusions and Discoveries: Studies on India in the British Imagination, 1880–1930* (1972) ch. vii.

June Perry Levine, *Creation and Criticism: E. M. Forster's 'A Passage to India'* (1971).

Jeffrey Meyers, *Fiction and the Colonial Experience* (1973) ch. ii.

(g) SYMBOLISM (CH. 2)

Austin Warren, *A Rage for Order* (Chicago, 1948).

Gertrude White, '*A Passage to India*, Analysis and Revaluation', *PMLA*, LXVIII (1953) 641–57.

Glen O. Allen, 'Structure, Symbol and Theme in E. M. Forster's *A Passage to India*', *PMLA*, LXX (1955).

Frank Kermode, 'The One Orderly Product (E. M. Forster)', in *Puzzles and Epiphanies. Essays and Reviews: 1958–1961* (1962).

(h) THE LANGUAGE OF THE NOVEL (CHS 4, 5, 6)

E. K. Brown, *Rhythm in the Novel* (Toronto, 1950).

Kenneth Burke, *Language as Symbolic Action* (Berkeley, Calif., 1966).

Alan Wilde, *Art and Order: A Study of E. M. Forster* (New York, 1965).

B. K. Das, 'A Stylistic Analysis of the Speech of the Indian Characters in Forster's *A Passage to India*', in *Focus on Forster's 'A Passage to India': Indian Essays in Criticism* ed. V. A. Shahane (Madras, 1975).

Michael Orange: 'Language and Silence in *A Passage to India*', in *E. M. Forster: A Human Exploration* [section (e) above].

P. N. Furbank, 'Forster and "Bloomsbury" Prose', ibid.

Barbara Rosecrance, '*A Passage to India*', *Forster's Narrative Vision* (Ithaca, NY, 1983).

(i) FORSTER'S IMAGINATIVE PHILOSOPHY (CHS 7, 8)

In addition to the works cited in the notes, other works dealing with some of the issues discussed are

John Beer, *The Achievement of E. M. Forster* (1962), for the role of the romantic imagination in Forster;

Barbara Hardy, *The Appropriate Form* (1964), for the supernatural;

John Colmer, *E. M. Forster: The Personal Voice* (1975), for the imagination;

M. M. Mahood, 'The Birth of Krishna: Forster's *A Passage to India*', in *The Colonial Encounter: A Reading of Six Novels* (1977), for Forster's mysticism.

The role of Professor Godbole has been examined in

James McConkey, *The Novels of E. M. Forster* (Ithaca, NY, 1957) pp. 132–60;

David Shustermann, 'The Curious Case of Professor Godbole: *A Passage to India* Re-examined', *PMLA* LXXVI (1961) 426–35;

T. G. Vaidyanathan, 'In Defence of Professor Godbole', in *Focus on Forster's 'A Passage to India': Indian Essays in Criticism*, ed. V. A. Shahane (Madras, 1975).

Index